Table of Contents

Introduction

Welcome to the comprehensive guide designed to help you master the Microsoft SC-900 exam and achieve your certification in Security, Compliance, and Identity Fundamentals. This book is your definitive resource, tailored to provide you with the knowledge and skills necessary to succeed in this foundational exam. Whether you are a business stakeholder, new or existing IT professional, or a student looking to expand your understanding of Microsoft's security solutions, this book will equip you with the tools to excel.

The SC-900 exam covers critical concepts in security, compliance, and identity, focusing on Microsoft's cloud-based and related services. This certification serves as a valuable credential, demonstrating your proficiency in these essential areas and your ability to apply this knowledge in real-world scenarios. By the end of this book, you will have a solid grasp of the core principles and practical applications, ready to tackle the exam with confidence.

Overview of the SC-900 Exam:

The Microsoft SC-900 exam is designed to validate your foundational knowledge in security, compliance, and identity within the context of Microsoft's services. This exam assesses your understanding of key concepts, the capabilities of Microsoft solutions, and the ability to implement these solutions effectively.

Exam Format and Structure:

The SC-900 exam consists of multiple-choice questions, case studies, and scenario-based questions. These questions are designed to test your comprehension of theoretical knowledge as well as practical applications. The exam typically includes:

- Multiple-choice questions: These questions test your understanding of core concepts and your ability to recall factual information.

- Case Studies: These are complex scenarios that require you to apply your knowledge to real-world situations.

- Scenario-Based Questions: These questions present specific situations where you must choose the best course of action based on the given context.

To pass the SC-900 exam, you need to achieve a score of at least 700 out of 1000. The exam is available in several languages, making it accessible to a global audience.

Key Areas Covered in the Exam:

1. Describe the Concepts of Security, Compliance, and Identity (10-15%): This section covers the fundamental principles of security, compliance, and identity

management. You'll learn the importance of protecting data and systems, adhering to regulatory requirements, and managing user identities.

2. Describe the Capabilities of Microsoft Entra (25-30%): This part focuses on Microsoft Entra's identity and access management capabilities. You'll explore authentication methods, access management, and identity protection features.

3. Describe the Capabilities of Microsoft Security Solutions (35-40%): This section delves into Microsoft's security solutions, including core infrastructure services like Azure Firewall, threat detection with Microsoft Sentinel, and threat protection with Microsoft Defender.

4. Describe the Capabilities of Microsoft Compliance Solutions (20-25%): Here, you'll learn about Microsoft's compliance tools, such as the Microsoft Service Trust Portal, Microsoft Purview Compliance Manager, and data governance solutions.

How This Book Will Help You Pass:

This book is structured to guide you through each topic with detailed explanations, practical examples, and real-world scenarios. By following the content and engaging with the practice questions and case studies provided, you will build a comprehensive understanding of the exam material. My optimistic and supportive approach is designed to boost your confidence and prepare you thoroughly for the exam day.

With dedication and the right resources, passing the SC-900 exam is within your reach. I have passed the exam myself so you are receiving first-hand knowledge of the exam. Use this book as your roadmap to certification success and take the first step towards advancing your career in the dynamic fields of security, compliance, and identity management.

Detailed Breakdown of Exam Objectives

Describe the Concepts of Security, Compliance, and Identity (10-15%)

Security Concepts:

Definition: Security involves protecting data and systems from unauthorized access and ensuring the confidentiality, integrity, and availability (CIA) of information. This triad is essential for safeguarding data and systems against threats like data breaches, cyber-attacks, and unauthorized access.

Importance: Security is fundamental to protecting an organization's assets, including its data, systems, and reputation. Without robust security measures, an organization is vulnerable to various threats, leading to potential financial loss, legal penalties, and damage to customer trust. Ensuring data confidentiality, integrity, and availability is crucial for maintaining operational stability and protecting sensitive information from malicious actors.

Examples:

1. Firewalls: These act as barriers between trusted internal networks and untrusted external networks (like the internet), filtering incoming and outgoing traffic based on predefined security rules.

2. Encryption: This converts data into a code to prevent unauthorized access. For instance, using SSL/TLS encryption for data in transit protects sensitive information transmitted over the internet.

3. Access Controls: These include mechanisms like user authentication and authorization to ensure that only authorized individuals can access specific resources. Role-Based Access Control (RBAC) assigns access permissions based on user roles within an organization.

Compliance Concepts:

Definition: Compliance refers to adhering to regulations, standards, and policies designed to protect data privacy and integrity. It involves implementing and following procedures that ensure an organization meets legal and regulatory requirements.

Importance: Compliance is critical for avoiding legal penalties, protecting the organization's reputation, and ensuring the privacy and security of sensitive information. It demonstrates a commitment to ethical practices and builds trust with customers and stakeholders. Non-compliance can result in hefty fines, legal action, and loss of business.

Examples:

1. GDPR (General Data Protection Regulation): This European regulation mandates strict data protection and privacy rules for individuals within the EU. Organizations

must comply with requirements such as data breach notifications and data subject rights.

2. HIPAA (Health Insurance Portability and Accountability Act): This U.S. regulation protects sensitive patient health information from being disclosed without the patient's consent or knowledge.

3. PCI DSS (Payment Card Industry Data Security Standard): This set of security standards is designed to ensure that all companies that accept, process, store, or transmit credit card information maintain a secure environment.

Identity Concepts:

Definition: Identity management involves verifying and managing users' identities and their access to resources. It ensures that individuals are who they claim to be and that they have appropriate access to organizational resources.

Importance: Identity management is essential for controlling access to sensitive data and resources, ensuring that only authorized users can access specific information. It helps prevent unauthorized access and potential security breaches, protecting the integrity and confidentiality of data.

Examples:

1. Multi-Factor Authentication (MFA): This security process requires users to provide two or more verification

factors to gain access to a resource, significantly enhancing security beyond just passwords.

2. Single Sign-On (SSO): This authentication process allows a user to access multiple applications with one set of login credentials, improving user convenience and security by reducing password fatigue and the risk of credential reuse.

Describe the Capabilities of Microsoft Entra (25-30%)

Function and Identity Types:

Microsoft Entra ID: This service manages identities and provides authentication capabilities, ensuring secure access to applications and resources.

Identity Types:

- User Identities: These are typically associated with individual users and are used to authenticate and authorize access to resources.

- Service Principal Identities: These identities are used by applications or services to authenticate and access specific resources.

- Managed Identities: These are automatically managed identities provided by Azure, used to simplify identity management for applications running on Azure services.

Hybrid Identity: This combines on-premises and cloud-based identity solutions, allowing for seamless integration and management of user identities across both environments. It enables organizations to maintain control over their identities while leveraging the benefits of the cloud.

Authentication Capabilities:

Authentication Methods: Microsoft Entra supports various authentication methods, including passwords, biometrics (such as fingerprint or facial recognition), and MFA. These methods enhance security by ensuring that users are properly authenticated before accessing resources.

Password Protection: This involves implementing policies and practices to secure passwords, such as enforcing strong password requirements, regular password changes, and using password managers to store and manage passwords securely.

Access Management Capabilities:

Conditional Access: Conditional Access policies control access to resources based on specific conditions, such as user location, device compliance, and risk level. These policies help enforce security measures dynamically, ensuring that access is granted only under secure conditions.

Role-Based Access Control (RBAC): RBAC assigns permissions based on user roles within the organization. This ensures that users have only the access necessary for their job functions, reducing the risk of unauthorized access.

Identity Protection and Governance:

Entra ID Governance: This manages the identity lifecycle and access, ensuring that user identities are properly managed and that access is granted and revoked as needed. It helps maintain compliance and security by managing access reviews and entitlements.

Privileged Identity Management: This feature manages and monitors elevated access, providing just-in-time privileged access and reducing the risk of excessive permissions. It ensures that privileged access is granted only when necessary and is closely monitored.

Describe the Capabilities of Microsoft Security Solutions (35-40%)

Core Infrastructure Security Services:

Azure DDoS Protection: This service protects applications from distributed denial-of-service attacks by monitoring and mitigating traffic anomalies. It ensures application availability and performance by blocking malicious traffic while allowing legitimate users to access the services.

Azure Firewall: Azure Firewall is a managed, cloud-based network security service that protects Azure Virtual Network resources. It provides network filtering to control traffic and includes logging and monitoring capabilities to enhance security visibility and compliance.

Web Application Firewall (WAF): A WAF protects web applications by filtering and monitoring HTTP traffic between a web application and the internet. It defends against common threats like SQL injection, cross-site scripting (XSS), and other web exploits by analyzing and filtering malicious traffic.

Security Management Capabilities

Microsoft Defender for Cloud: This service provides unified security management and advanced threat protection across hybrid cloud environments. Key features include continuous security assessment, threat detection, and automated response capabilities to protect resources and workloads.

Cloud Security Posture Management (CSPM): CSPM tools assess and improve an organization's security posture by continuously monitoring, identifying, and remediating security risks. It provides visibility into misconfigurations and compliance violations, ensuring that cloud environments are secure and compliant.

Capabilities of Microsoft Sentinel:

SIEM and SOAR: Security Information and Event Management (SIEM) and Security Orchestration Automated Response (SOAR) provide threat detection and response capabilities. SIEM collects and analyzes security data to identify potential threats, while SOAR automates response actions to mitigate incidents quickly.

Threat Detection: This capability involves identifying and mitigating security threats using advanced analytics and machine learning. It helps organizations detect suspicious activities and respond to potential threats in real time.

Threat Protection with Microsoft Defender XDR:

Defender Services: Microsoft Defender includes services for Office 365, Endpoint, Cloud Apps, and Identity. These services provide comprehensive threat protection across different environments, ensuring that users and resources are secure.

Vulnerability Management: This involves identifying and managing vulnerabilities across endpoints. Microsoft Defender Vulnerability Management continuously assesses and prioritizes vulnerabilities, providing remediation recommendations to reduce risks.

Describe the Capabilities of Microsoft Compliance Solutions (20-25%)

Microsoft Service Trust Portal and Privacy Principles:

Service Trust Portal: This portal provides access to compliance and privacy resources, including compliance documentation, audit reports, and trust resources. It helps organizations understand and meet regulatory requirements.

Privacy Principles: These principles outline Microsoft's approach to data privacy and protection. They include commitments to data transparency, security, and user control, ensuring that personal data is handled responsibly and in compliance with privacy regulations.

Compliance Management with Microsoft Purview:

Purview Compliance Portal: This centralized platform provides tools for managing compliance across the organization. It helps organizations assess compliance status, identify gaps, and implement controls to ensure adherence to regulatory requirements.

Compliance Manager: This tool helps manage and assess compliance status, providing insights into compliance risks and offering recommendations for improvement. It supports various regulations and standards, helping organizations maintain compliance.

Information Protection and Data Governance:

Data Classification: Tools for categorizing data based on sensitivity help organizations apply appropriate security and compliance controls. Data classification ensures that sensitive information is protected and handled according to its classification.

Sensitivity Labels: These labels apply security policies based on data sensitivity. They help enforce encryption, access restrictions, and data loss prevention (DLP) policies, ensuring that sensitive data is protected.

Data Loss Prevention (DLP): DLP tools help prevent data breaches by identifying and blocking unauthorized data transfers. They ensure that sensitive information is not leaked or mishandled, protecting against accidental or malicious data loss.

Insider Risk, eDiscovery, and Audit:

Insider Risk Management: Tools for managing and mitigating insider threats help organizations detect and respond to potential risks from within. Insider Risk Management involves monitoring user activities and identifying behaviors that may indicate a threat.

eDiscovery: eDiscovery tools help organizations find and manage electronic information for legal and regulatory investigations. They support the collection, preservation, and analysis of data, ensuring that relevant information is available and protected.

Audit Solutions: Audit tools track and audit user activities, providing detailed logs and reports. These logs help organizations monitor compliance, investigate security incidents, and ensure accountability by providing a clear record of actions taken within the environment.

10 Entry-Level Jobs

1. Security Analyst

A Security Analyst is responsible for monitoring and analyzing security events to identify potential threats, investigating security breaches, and implementing protective measures. For example, using Security Information and Event Management (SIEM) tools, they can track and respond to suspicious activities. They might conduct vulnerability assessments to identify weaknesses in the IT infrastructure and develop security policies to mitigate these risks. In a job scenario, a Security Analyst might discover unusual login patterns in the SIEM tool, indicating a potential brute-force attack. They would then investigate this activity, confirm the breach, and implement additional security controls such as enhancing password policies or deploying multi-factor authentication (MFA) to prevent future incidents. Their work is crucial in ensuring the organization's IT infrastructure is protected from cyber threats, and maintaining the integrity and confidentiality of sensitive data.

2. Compliance Analyst

A Compliance Analyst ensures that an organization complies with regulatory requirements and internal policies. They conduct audits, prepare compliance reports, and stay updated with changes in laws and regulations. For instance, they might review the company's data handling practices to ensure compliance with the General Data Protection Regulation (GDPR). In a practical scenario, a Compliance Analyst might discover that the organization is not fully compliant with GDPR due to inadequate data protection measures. They would then develop and implement a plan to address these gaps, such as enhancing encryption protocols and updating privacy policies. By maintaining compliance with relevant regulations, they help prevent legal issues and fines, protecting the organization from potential penalties and reputational damage.

3. Identity and Access Management (IAM) Specialist

An IAM Specialist manages user identities and controls access to systems and data. They implement MFA, manage user access permissions, and conduct access reviews. In a real-world scenario, they might find that some employees have access to sensitive data that is not required for their roles. The IAM Specialist would then adjust access permissions, ensuring that employees have only the access necessary for their job functions. They might also conduct regular access reviews to identify and rectify any discrepancies. Their role is vital in ensuring that only authorized users can access sensitive information and systems, reducing the risk of unauthorized access and potential data breaches.

4. Security Operations Center (SOC) Analyst

A SOC Analyst monitors and responds to security incidents in real time. They analyze security alerts, perform initial triage on incidents, and coordinate with incident response teams. For example, during a cybersecurity incident such as a malware outbreak, the SOC Analyst would detect the threat through security alerts, assess the impact, and initiate containment measures. They might isolate affected systems and work with the incident response team to eradicate the malware and restore normal operations. Their quick response and thorough analysis provide the first line of defense against security threats, minimizing damage and ensuring the organization can continue its operations securely.

5. Data Privacy Officer

A Data Privacy Officer oversees the organization's data privacy policies and practices. They conduct data protection impact assessments, manage data breaches, and ensure compliance with data privacy laws like GDPR. In a job scenario, they might identify a data handling process that exposes personal data to unnecessary risks. The Data Privacy Officer would then recommend and implement changes to this process, such as improving encryption methods and training employees on data privacy best practices. By protecting personal data and ensuring compliance with privacy regulations, they safeguard the organization's reputation and avoid legal repercussions.

6. IT Auditor

An IT Auditor evaluates the effectiveness of an organization's IT controls and processes. They perform audits on IT systems, review access controls, and make recommendations for improvements. For instance, during an audit, they might discover that certain critical systems lack adequate access controls. The IT Auditor would then recommend implementing stricter access controls and conducting regular reviews to ensure compliance. Their work is essential in identifying weaknesses in IT controls, helping mitigate risks, and ensuring that the organization's IT environment is secure and efficient.

7. Cloud Security Specialist

A Cloud Security Specialist secures cloud-based systems and data. They implement cloud security policies, manage cloud security tools, and conduct security assessments for cloud environments. For example, they might discover that certain cloud services are misconfigured, leading to potential vulnerabilities. The Cloud Security Specialist would then reconfigure these services to align with best security practices, implement monitoring tools to detect any anomalies, and conduct regular security assessments to ensure the cloud environment remains secure. Their role is crucial in ensuring the security of data and applications in the cloud, and protecting against breaches and data loss.

8. Security Consultant

A Security Consultant provides expert advice on security best practices and solutions. They conduct risk assessments, develop security strategies, and assist with security implementations. In a job scenario, a Security Consultant might be hired to assess a company's overall security posture. They would identify potential risks, such as outdated software or insufficient access controls, and develop a comprehensive security strategy to address these issues. This might include recommending the implementation of advanced security measures like MFA, encryption, and continuous monitoring. By providing tailored security solutions, they help organizations improve their security posture and protect against potential threats.

9. Incident Responder

An Incident Responder responds to and mitigates security incidents. They investigate security breaches, coordinate incident response efforts, and document incidents. For example, during a ransomware attack, the Incident Responder would analyze the breach, identify the entry point, and work to contain the threat. They would coordinate with IT and security teams to restore affected systems and data from backups. After the incident is resolved, they would document the event and conduct a post-incident analysis to improve future response efforts. Their role is critical in minimizing the impact of security incidents and ensuring that normal operations can resume quickly.

10. Security Compliance Specialist

A Security Compliance Specialist ensures that security practices comply with industry standards and regulations. They review security policies, conduct compliance audits, and manage compliance documentation. In a real-world scenario, they might find that the organization is not fully compliant with industry standards such as ISO/IEC 27001. The Security Compliance Specialist would then develop a plan to address these gaps, including updating security policies, conducting training sessions for employees, and implementing necessary controls. By maintaining regulatory compliance, they help protect the organization from penalties and breaches, ensuring a secure and compliant IT environment.

Sample Questions & Answers

Concepts of Security, Compliance, and Identity:

1. What is the CIA triad in information security?

The CIA triad stands for Confidentiality, Integrity, and Availability. Confidentiality ensures that data is accessible only to those authorized to have access. Integrity ensures that data is accurate and reliable. Availability ensures that data and systems are accessible when needed.

2. Why is data encryption important for data security?

Encryption transforms readable data into an unreadable format, which protects it from unauthorized access. It ensures that even if data is intercepted or accessed without authorization, it remains protected and unusable to unauthorized individuals.

3. What is a security policy?

A security policy is a formal document that outlines how an organization will protect its IT assets and data. It includes guidelines on access control, data protection, and incident response.

4. Define the concept of least privilege.

The principle of least privilege involves granting users the minimum level of access necessary to perform their job functions. This minimizes potential damage from accidents, misuse, or malicious activities.

5. What is multi-factor authentication (MFA) and why is it important?

MFA requires users to provide two or more verification factors to gain access to a resource. This significantly reduces the risk of unauthorized access as it adds an extra layer of security beyond just passwords.

6. How does an organization benefit from security awareness training?

Security awareness training educates employees about cybersecurity threats and best practices. It helps create a security-conscious culture, reducing the risk of human error and enhancing overall security posture.

7. Explain the concept of data integrity.

Data integrity ensures that information remains accurate and consistent over its lifecycle. This is important to maintain the trustworthiness and reliability of data.

8. What is a threat model?

A threat model is a structured representation of potential security threats to a system. It helps in identifying, understanding, and mitigating potential risks.

9. Why is incident response planning crucial for organizations?

Incident response planning ensures that organizations can effectively manage and mitigate the impact of security incidents. It provides a structured approach for identifying, responding to, and recovering from incidents.

10. Describe the role of access control in security.

Access control determines who is allowed to access and use resources in a computing environment. It is crucial for protecting sensitive information and systems from unauthorized access.

11. What are the main objectives of compliance in information security?

Compliance aims to ensure that an organization meets regulatory requirements and industry standards. It helps protect data, reduce legal risks, and build trust with stakeholders.

12. What is the difference between a vulnerability and a threat?

A vulnerability is a weakness in a system that can be exploited. A threat is a potential cause of an unwanted impact to a system. Understanding both helps in identifying and mitigating risks.

13. What is a security audit?

A security audit is a systematic evaluation of an organization's information system security. It assesses how well security policies are being followed and identifies areas for improvement.

14. Explain the importance of data backup.

Data backup involves copying and storing data to protect against data loss. It ensures that data can be restored in the event of hardware failure, cyber-attacks, or other data loss incidents.

15. What is the purpose of a firewall in network security?

A firewall is a security device that monitors and controls incoming and outgoing network traffic based on predetermined security rules. It acts as a barrier between a trusted network and untrusted networks.

16. How does role-based access control (RBAC) enhance security?

RBAC assigns permissions based on user roles, ensuring that individuals only have access to the resources necessary for their job. This reduces the risk of unauthorized access.

17. What is the significance of a security operations center (SOC)?

A SOC is a centralized unit that monitors, detects, and responds to security incidents. It helps ensure continuous security monitoring and a coordinated response to threats.

18. Describe the concept of data classification.

Data classification involves categorizing data based on its sensitivity and the level of protection it requires. This helps in implementing appropriate security measures for different types of data.

19. What is identity management?

Identity management involves verifying and managing user identities and their access to resources. It ensures that only authorized users can access sensitive information and systems.

20. Explain the role of encryption in protecting data at rest.

Encryption transforms data into an unreadable format when it is stored. This protects the data from unauthorized access, ensuring its confidentiality and integrity.

21. What are the main types of security controls?

Security controls can be preventive, detective, and corrective. Preventive controls aim to prevent security incidents, detective controls identify and detect incidents, and corrective controls respond to and mitigate the effects of incidents.

22. What is the purpose of a data breach notification policy?

A data breach notification policy outlines the procedures for notifying affected parties and regulatory bodies in the event of a data breach. It ensures timely and effective communication to mitigate the impact of the breach.

23. Why is it important to regularly update and patch systems?

Regular updates and patches fix security vulnerabilities and improve system stability. This helps protect against cyber attacks that exploit known vulnerabilities.

24. Explain the importance of a business continuity plan (BCP).

A BCP ensures that critical business functions can continue during and after a disaster. It helps minimize downtime and protect against financial and reputational damage.

25. What is the role of an IT auditor in security compliance?

An IT auditor assesses the effectiveness of an organization's IT controls and compliance with regulations. They identify weaknesses and recommend improvements to enhance security and compliance.

Capabilities of Microsoft Entra:

26. What is Microsoft Entra ID?

Microsoft Entra ID is a cloud-based identity and access management service. It provides features like user authentication, single sign-on (SSO), and multi-factor authentication (MFA) to secure access to applications and data.

27. Explain the concept of hybrid identity.

Hybrid identity involves integrating on-premises and cloud-based identity solutions. This allows organizations to manage user identities across both environments seamlessly.

28. What are the different types of identities in Microsoft Entra?

Types of identities in Microsoft Entra include user identities, service principal identities, and managed identities. Each type serves a different purpose and has specific management requirements.

29. How does Conditional Access enhance security in Microsoft Entra?

Conditional Access uses policies to control access to resources based on conditions like user location, device status, and risk level. This helps enforce security measures dynamically based on context.

30. What is the purpose of Microsoft Entra ID Governance?

Microsoft Entra ID Governance manages the identity lifecycle, ensuring that users have appropriate access throughout their employment. It helps maintain compliance and security by managing access reviews and entitlements.

31. Describe the capabilities of Microsoft Entra Privileged Identity Management (PIM).

PIM helps manage, control, and monitor access to critical resources. It provides just-in-time privileged access, reduces the risk of excessive permissions, and improves security compliance.

32. What is the role of Microsoft Entra ID Protection?

Microsoft Entra ID Protection uses machine learning to detect and respond to suspicious activities. It helps protect user identities by identifying potential security risks and automatically enforcing policies to mitigate them.

33. Explain the concept of single sign-on (SSO) in Microsoft Entra.

SSO allows users to authenticate once and gain access to multiple applications without needing to re-enter credentials. This improves user experience and reduces the risk of password fatigue.

34. How does Microsoft Entra Permissions Management enhance security?

Permissions Management provides visibility and control over permissions across cloud environments. It helps enforce the principle of least privilege and ensures that access is granted only as needed.

35. What are access reviews in Microsoft Entra?

Access reviews are periodic evaluations of user access to ensure that permissions are appropriate and up-to-date. They help identify and remove unnecessary access, improving security and compliance.

36. How does Microsoft Entra integrate with other Microsoft services?

Microsoft Entra integrates with services like Microsoft 365, Azure, and Dynamics 365 to provide seamless identity and access management. This integration enhances security and simplifies user management across the Microsoft ecosystem.

37. What is the purpose of authentication methods in Microsoft Entra?

Authentication methods in Microsoft Entra include passwords, biometrics, and MFA. They provide various options for verifying user identities and ensuring secure access to resources.

38. Explain the concept of password protection and management in Microsoft Entra.

Password protection and management involve implementing policies to ensure strong, unique passwords and reducing the risk of password-related security incidents. Features like password expiration, complexity requirements, and self-service password reset enhance security.

39. What is the role of Microsoft Entra roles and role-based access control (RBAC)?

RBAC assigns permissions based on roles within Microsoft Entra. This ensures that users have access only to the resources necessary for their job which reduces the risk of unauthorized access

40. What is Microsoft Entra Identity Governance and its benefits?

Microsoft Entra Identity Governance helps organizations manage identity lifecycle, entitlements, and compliance. It provides tools for access reviews, ensuring that users' access rights are periodically reviewed and updated to prevent unauthorized access. Benefits include improved security, compliance with regulatory requirements, and streamlined user access management.

41. Explain the importance of multi-factor authentication (MFA) in Microsoft Entra.

MFA is crucial because it adds an extra layer of security beyond just passwords, requiring users to provide multiple verification methods. This significantly reduces the risk of unauthorized access due to compromised credentials, thereby protecting sensitive information and resources.

42. What are the key features of Microsoft Entra Privileged Identity Management (PIM)?

PIM offers features like just-in-time privileged access, access reviews, and audit logs. It controls and monitors access to critical resources, ensuring that privileged access is granted only when necessary and monitored to prevent abuse.

43. How does Microsoft Entra ID Protection detect and respond to suspicious activities?

Microsoft Entra ID Protection uses machine learning algorithms to analyze user behavior and detect anomalies indicative of potential security threats. When suspicious activities are detected, it can automatically enforce policies such as requiring MFA or blocking access to mitigate risks.

44. What are the benefits of using Microsoft Entra Permissions Management?

Permissions Management provides visibility into permissions across cloud environments, helping organizations enforce least privilege principles. It reduces the risk of over-privileged access and ensures that permissions are granted only as needed, enhancing security and compliance.

45. Describe the integration of Microsoft Entra with other security solutions like Microsoft Defender.

Microsoft Entra integrates with Microsoft Defender to provide comprehensive security solutions. This integration allows for unified threat detection and response, streamlined identity and access management, and enhanced protection across Microsoft environments.

46. What is the role of Conditional Access policies in Microsoft Entra?

Conditional Access policies control access to resources based on specific conditions like user location, device health, and risk level. These policies help enforce security measures dynamically, ensuring that access is granted only under secure conditions.

47. How does Microsoft Entra support hybrid identity scenarios?

Microsoft Entra supports hybrid identity by integrating on-premises Active Directory with Azure Active Directory.

This allows for seamless identity management across on-premises and cloud environments, providing a unified approach to user authentication and access control.

48. What are the different types of access reviews available in Microsoft Entra?

Microsoft Entra offers various access reviews, including user access reviews, application access reviews, and group membership reviews. These reviews help ensure that permissions remain appropriate and up-to-date, reducing the risk of unauthorized access.

49. Explain the concept of identity lifecycle management in Microsoft Entra.

Identity lifecycle management involves managing user identities from creation to deactivation. Microsoft Entra provides tools for automating user provisioning, updating access rights based on role changes, and de-provisioning users when they leave the organization, ensuring secure and efficient identity management.

50. What is Microsoft Entra ID and how does it enhance security?

Microsoft Entra ID is a cloud-based identity and access management service that enhances security by providing features like user authentication, SSO, and MFA. It helps organizations manage and secure access to applications and data, ensuring that only authorized users can access sensitive resources.

51. How does Microsoft Entra help with regulatory compliance?

Microsoft Entra helps organizations meet regulatory compliance by providing tools for managing access controls, conducting access reviews, and generating audit reports. These capabilities ensure that organizations can demonstrate compliance with regulations such as GDPR, HIPAA, and SOX.

52. What is the importance of user authentication in Microsoft Entra?

User authentication is crucial in Microsoft Entra as it verifies the identity of users before granting access to resources. It ensures that only authorized users can access sensitive data and systems, protecting against unauthorized access and potential security breaches.

53. How does Microsoft Entra handle password protection and management?

Microsoft Entra implements policies for password protection and management, including enforcing password complexity requirements, expiration policies, and self-service password reset options. These measures help enhance security by ensuring strong, unique passwords and reducing the risk of password-related incidents.

54. Explain the concept of single sign-on (SSO) and its benefits in Microsoft Entra.

SSO allows users to authenticate once and gain access to multiple applications without needing to re-enter credentials. This improves user experience by reducing the number of logins required and enhances security by minimizing password fatigue and reducing the risk of credential reuse.

55. What are the benefits of using Microsoft Entra ID Protection?

Microsoft Entra ID Protection benefits include real-time detection of suspicious activities, automatic enforcement of security policies, and detailed risk analysis. These capabilities help protect user identities and reduce the risk of unauthorized access and identity-related security incidents.

Describe the Capabilities of Microsoft Security Solutions:

56. What is Azure Distributed Denial-of-Service (DDoS) Protection and its purpose?

Azure DDoS Protection safeguards applications from DDoS attacks by monitoring and mitigating traffic anomalies. It ensures application availability and performance by automatically blocking malicious traffic while allowing legitimate users to access the services.

57. Explain the function of Azure Firewall in network security.

Azure Firewall is a managed cloud-based network security service that protects Azure Virtual Network resources. It provides network filtering to control traffic, logging, and monitoring capabilities to enhance security visibility and compliance.

58. What is a Web Application Firewall (WAF) and how does it protect applications?

A WAF protects web applications by filtering and monitoring HTTP traffic between a web application and the internet. It defends against common threats like SQL injection, cross-site scripting (XSS), and other web exploits by analyzing and filtering malicious traffic.

59. How does network segmentation with Azure Virtual Networks enhance security?

Network segmentation involves dividing a network into smaller segments to control traffic flow and limit the spread of threats. Azure Virtual Networks provide network isolation and segmentation, ensuring that sensitive data and applications are protected from unauthorized access and lateral movement.

60. Describe the role of Network Security Groups (NSGs) in Azure.

NSGs control inbound and outbound traffic to Azure resources by defining security rules. These rules filter network traffic based on IP addresses, ports, and protocols, helping secure Azure Virtual Networks and protecting resources from unauthorized access.

61. What is Azure Bastion and its purpose?

Azure Bastion provides secure and seamless RDP and SSH connectivity to Azure Virtual Machines directly through the Azure portal. It eliminates the need for public IP addresses and VPNs, reducing the attack surface and enhancing security.

62. Explain the capabilities of Azure Key Vault.

Azure Key Vault securely stores and manages sensitive information like secrets, keys, and certificates. It provides centralized management, access control, and logging, ensuring that sensitive data is protected and access is tightly controlled.

63. What is Microsoft Defender for Cloud and its key features?

Microsoft Defender for Cloud provides unified security management and advanced threat protection across hybrid cloud environments. Key features include continuous security assessment, threat detection, and automated response capabilities to protect resources and workloads.

64. How does Cloud Security Posture Management (CSPM) improve security?

CSPM helps organizations manage and improve their cloud security posture by continuously monitoring, identifying, and remediating security risks. It provides visibility into misconfigurations and compliance violations, ensuring that cloud environments are secure and compliant.

65. Describe the purpose of Microsoft Sentinel in security operations.

Microsoft Sentinel is a cloud-native Security Information and Event Management (SIEM) solution that provides intelligent security analytics and threat intelligence. It helps detect, investigate, and respond to security threats, enhancing security operations and reducing response times.

66. What is the role of threat detection in Microsoft Sentinel?

Threat detection in Microsoft Sentinel involves analyzing security data to identify potential threats and anomalies. It uses machine learning and threat intelligence to detect suspicious activities and generate alerts for further investigation and response.

67. Explain the concept of security orchestration, automation, and response (SOAR) in Microsoft Sentinel.

SOAR capabilities in Microsoft Sentinel automate repetitive security tasks, orchestrate workflows, and enable rapid response to security incidents. This improves efficiency, reduces manual efforts, and ensures timely and consistent incident handling.

68. How does Microsoft Defender for Office 365 enhance email security?

Microsoft Defender for Office 365 protects against email-based threats like phishing, malware, and spam. It provides advanced threat protection, safe links and attachments, and anti-phishing policies to secure email communications and prevent attacks.

69. What is Microsoft Defender for Endpoint and its key features?

Microsoft Defender for Endpoint provides endpoint protection and advanced threat detection. Key features include endpoint detection and response (EDR), automated investigation and remediation, and threat intelligence integration to protect against sophisticated cyber threats.

70. How does Microsoft Defender for Cloud Apps enhance security for cloud applications?

Microsoft Defender for Cloud Apps provides visibility and control over cloud applications and services. It helps detect and respond to threats, enforce data protection policies, and manage application usage to ensure security and compliance in the cloud.

71. Describe the purpose of Microsoft Defender for Identity.

Microsoft Defender for Identity helps protect on-premises Active Directory from identity-based threats. It uses behavioral analytics to detect suspicious activities, compromised accounts, and lateral movement, providing insights into potential identity-related security incidents.

72. What is Microsoft Defender Vulnerability Management and its benefits?

Microsoft Defender Vulnerability Management identifies and mitigates vulnerabilities across endpoints. It continuously assesses and prioritizes vulnerabilities, providing remediation recommendations to reduce risks. Benefits include proactive vulnerability management, improved security posture, and reduced exposure to potential attacks.

73. How does Azure Security Center help secure cloud resources?

Azure Security Center provides a unified security management system for hybrid cloud workloads. It offers continuous security assessments, advanced threat protection, and automated remediation. This helps ensure that cloud resources are secure and compliant with organizational policies and regulatory requirements.

74. What is Azure Policy, and how does it enforce compliance?

Azure Policy allows organizations to create, assign, and manage policies that enforce rules and effects over their Azure resources. It ensures resources stay compliant with corporate standards by evaluating resources and taking corrective actions when non-compliant resources are found.

75. Explain the concept of security posture management in Azure.

Security posture management in Azure involves continuously assessing and improving the security status of Azure resources. Tools like Azure Security Center provide visibility into security posture, identify misconfigurations, and offer recommendations for remediation to enhance overall security.

76. How does Microsoft Defender for Identity detect and respond to lateral movement attacks?

Microsoft Defender for Identity uses advanced analytics to detect suspicious activities indicative of lateral movement attacks, such as abnormal access patterns and credential usage. It provides alerts and detailed reports, enabling security teams to investigate and respond to potential threats promptly.

77. Describe the role of automated threat response in Microsoft security solutions.

Automated threat response uses machine learning and automation to detect, investigate, and respond to security incidents. It reduces the time to mitigate threats, minimizes human error, and ensures consistent and timely responses to security events.

78. What is Microsoft Cloud App Security, and what are its key features?

Microsoft Cloud App Security (MCAS) is a Cloud Access Security Broker (CASB) that provides visibility and control over user activities in cloud applications. Key features include threat detection, data protection, and compliance management to secure cloud usage and prevent data breaches.

79. How does Microsoft Defender for Office 365 protect against phishing attacks?

Microsoft Defender for Office 365 uses advanced algorithms to detect and block phishing attempts. It provides real-time protection through features like Safe Links and Safe Attachments, which scan and neutralize malicious content before it reaches users.

80. Explain the importance of security monitoring and logging in Azure.

Security monitoring and logging in Azure involve collecting and analyzing logs from various resources to detect and investigate security incidents. Tools like Azure Monitor and Azure Log Analytics provide visibility into security events, helping identify threats and maintain compliance with security policies.

81. What is the purpose of Azure AD Identity Protection?

Azure AD Identity Protection helps organizations detect and respond to identity-based risks. It uses machine learning to analyze user behaviors, identify anomalies, and enforce conditional access policies to mitigate risks associated with compromised identities.

82. How does Microsoft Defender for Endpoint integrate with other Microsoft security solutions?

Microsoft Defender for Endpoint integrates with solutions like Microsoft Defender for Office 365, Azure Security Center, and Microsoft Cloud App Security. This integration provides a unified security approach, enabling comprehensive threat detection, investigation, and response across endpoints and cloud environments.

83. Describe the concept of endpoint detection and response (EDR) in Microsoft Defender.

EDR in Microsoft Defender involves continuous monitoring and analysis of endpoint activities to detect and respond to advanced threats. It uses behavioral analytics to identify suspicious patterns, provides alerts, and offers automated remediation to mitigate potential security incidents.

84. What is the role of threat intelligence in Microsoft security solutions?

Threat intelligence in Microsoft security solutions involves collecting and analyzing data on emerging threats. This information helps enhance detection capabilities, inform security policies, and improve response strategies, ensuring that organizations stay ahead of evolving cyber threats.

85. How does Microsoft Sentinel use machine learning to enhance security?

Microsoft Sentinel uses machine learning to analyze security data, detect anomalies, and identify potential threats. It provides advanced analytics and automated threat detection, reducing the time to detect and respond to security incidents and improving overall security operations.

86. Explain the importance of continuous security assessment in Azure Security Center.

Continuous security assessment in Azure Security Center involves regularly evaluating the security posture of Azure resources. It helps identify vulnerabilities, misconfigurations, and compliance issues, providing actionable recommendations to enhance security and reduce risks.

87. What is the purpose of threat hunting in Microsoft security solutions?

Threat hunting involves proactively searching for hidden threats and potential vulnerabilities within an organization's environment. Microsoft security solutions provide tools and capabilities for threat hunting, enabling security teams to identify and mitigate threats before they can cause harm.

88. How does Microsoft Defender for Cloud Apps enforce data protection policies?

Microsoft Defender for Cloud Apps enforces data protection policies by monitoring and controlling data transfers, applying encryption, and preventing unauthorized access. It helps ensure that sensitive data is protected in cloud applications and complies with organizational and regulatory requirements.

89. What are the key features of Microsoft Defender for Identity?

Key features of Microsoft Defender for Identity include advanced threat detection, behavioral analytics, and real-time monitoring. It helps protect against identity-based attacks by identifying suspicious activities, compromised accounts, and lateral movement within the network.

90. How does Azure Key Vault manage and secure cryptographic keys?

Azure Key Vault securely stores and manages cryptographic keys, secrets, and certificates. It provides centralized management, access control, and logging, ensuring that sensitive information is protected and access is tightly controlled to prevent unauthorized use.

Capabilities of Microsoft Compliance Solutions:

91. What is the Microsoft Service Trust Portal?

The Microsoft Service Trust Portal provides access to information about Microsoft's security, privacy, and compliance practices. It includes compliance documentation, audit reports, and trust resources to help organizations understand and meet regulatory requirements.

92. How does Microsoft Purview Compliance Manager help organizations?

Microsoft Purview Compliance Manager provides tools for managing compliance with regulatory requirements. It helps organizations assess compliance status, identify gaps, and implement controls to ensure adherence to standards like GDPR, HIPAA, and ISO/IEC 27001.

93. Explain the concept of data classification in Microsoft Purview.

Data classification in Microsoft Purview involves categorizing data based on its sensitivity and value. It helps organizations apply appropriate security and compliance controls to protect sensitive information and ensure compliance with data protection regulations.

94. What are sensitivity labels in Microsoft Purview, and how are they used?

Sensitivity labels in Microsoft Purview are used to classify and protect data based on its sensitivity. Labels can be applied to documents, emails, and other data, enforcing encryption, access restrictions, and data loss prevention (DLP) policies to ensure data security.

95. How does Microsoft Purview help with data lifecycle management?

Microsoft Purview provides tools for managing the entire data lifecycle, from creation to deletion. It includes features like retention policies, records management, and automated data classification to ensure that data is managed securely and in compliance with regulatory requirements.

96. Describe the purpose of data loss prevention (DLP) in Microsoft Purview.

DLP in Microsoft Purview helps prevent the unauthorized sharing of sensitive information. It identifies and blocks data transfers that violate organizational policies, protecting data from accidental or malicious leaks and ensuring compliance with data protection regulations.

97. What is the role of Microsoft Priva in data privacy management?

Microsoft Priva helps organizations manage and protect personal data. It provides tools for data discovery, classification, and governance, ensuring that personal data is handled in compliance with privacy regulations like GDPR and CCPA.

98. How does Microsoft Purview handle eDiscovery and legal hold?

Microsoft Purview provides eDiscovery and legal hold capabilities to help organizations manage legal and regulatory investigations. It enables the collection, preservation, and analysis of electronic information, ensuring that relevant data is available and protected during legal proceedings.

99. Explain the importance of audit capabilities in Microsoft Purview.

Audit capabilities in Microsoft Purview provide detailed logs and reports of user activities and data

101. What is the Compliance Score in Microsoft Purview Compliance Manager and how is it calculated?

The Compliance Score in Microsoft Purview Compliance Manager provides a measure of an organization's compliance posture against regulatory requirements. It is calculated based on the completion of recommended actions that help mitigate compliance risks. Each action is assigned a point value, and the score is a percentage of points achieved out of the total possible points.

102. How does Microsoft Purview help in managing data subject requests?

Microsoft Purview assists in managing data subject requests by providing tools to discover, classify, and retrieve personal data across the organization. This ensures that organizations can efficiently respond to requests such as access, correction, deletion, or data portability, in compliance with regulations like GDPR.

103. What are retention policies in Microsoft Purview and how are they used?

Retention policies in Microsoft Purview are rules that govern how long data should be kept and when it should be deleted. These policies help ensure compliance with regulatory requirements and organizational data governance practices by automatically retaining or deleting data based on predefined criteria.

104. How does Microsoft Purview support regulatory compliance for industry-specific standards?

Microsoft Purview supports regulatory compliance for industry-specific standards by providing pre-built assessment templates and controls for various regulations, such as GDPR, HIPAA, and ISO/IEC 27001. These tools help organizations implement necessary controls and monitor compliance.

105. Explain the role of Microsoft Compliance Manager in risk assessment.

Microsoft Compliance Manager helps organizations assess compliance risks by providing insights into compliance status, identifying gaps, and recommending actions to mitigate risks. It offers a centralized view of compliance activities, allowing organizations to prioritize and address areas of high risk.

106. How does Microsoft Purview handle records management?

Microsoft Purview handles records management by providing tools to classify, retain, and dispose of records according to regulatory and organizational requirements. It ensures that records are managed throughout their lifecycle, from creation to disposal, in a secure and compliant manner.

107. What is the purpose of sensitivity label policies in Microsoft Purview?

Sensitivity label policies in Microsoft Purview define how sensitivity labels should be applied and enforced across an organization. These policies help ensure consistent data protection practices by automatically applying labels based on data content, user actions, or organizational rules.

108. How does Microsoft Purview help with managing insider risks?

Microsoft Purview helps manage insider risks by providing tools to monitor user activities, detect suspicious behavior, and enforce policies to prevent data leaks or unauthorized access. Insider Risk Management capabilities enable organizations to identify and mitigate potential threats from within.

109. What is the significance of the Microsoft Compliance Center dashboard?

The Microsoft Compliance Center dashboard provides a centralized view of an organization's compliance status, activities, and risks. It offers insights into compliance posture, active alerts, and recommended actions, helping organizations stay informed and proactive in managing compliance.

110. How does Microsoft Purview facilitate collaboration on compliance efforts?

Microsoft Purview facilitates collaboration on compliance efforts by providing shared workspaces, centralized documentation, and role-based access controls. This enables compliance teams to work together efficiently, track progress, and ensure that all stakeholders are informed and involved in compliance activities.

111. What are data protection impact assessments (DPIAs) and how does Microsoft Purview assist in conducting them?

Data Protection Impact Assessments (DPIAs) are evaluations required under GDPR to identify and mitigate risks associated with data processing activities. Microsoft Purview assists in conducting DPIAs by providing tools to document processing activities, assess risks, and implement necessary controls to protect personal data.

112. How does Microsoft Purview support automated compliance reporting?

Microsoft Purview supports automated compliance reporting by generating detailed reports based on compliance activities, risk assessments, and audit logs. These reports provide insights into compliance status, help track progress, and demonstrate adherence to regulatory requirements.

113. Explain the role of audit logs in Microsoft Purview.

Audit logs in Microsoft Purview track and record user activities, data access, and changes within the system. These logs provide a detailed audit trail that helps organizations monitor compliance, investigate incidents, and ensure accountability by documenting actions taken within the environment.

114. How does Microsoft Purview help organizations prepare for compliance audits?

Microsoft Purview helps organizations prepare for compliance audits by providing tools to document compliance activities, generate reports, and conduct self-assessments. It centralizes compliance documentation and tracks progress, ensuring that organizations are ready to demonstrate compliance during audits.

115. What is the significance of content explorer in Microsoft Purview?

Content Explorer in Microsoft Purview provides a detailed view of where sensitive information is stored and how it is being used. This tool helps organizations identify and manage sensitive data, apply appropriate protection measures, and ensure compliance with data protection regulations.

116. How does Microsoft Purview handle the enforcement of data residency requirements?

Microsoft Purview handles data residency requirements by providing tools to manage data storage locations and ensure that data remains within specified geographic boundaries. It helps organizations comply with regulations that mandate where data can be stored and processed.

117. Explain the concept of automated data classification in Microsoft Purview.

Automated data classification in Microsoft Purview involves using machine learning and predefined rules to identify and categorize data based on its content and sensitivity. This helps ensure that sensitive information is properly protected and managed according to compliance requirements.

118. How does Microsoft Purview ensure data integrity and confidentiality during eDiscovery processes?

Microsoft Purview ensures data integrity and confidentiality during eDiscovery processes by providing secure tools for data collection, preservation, and analysis. It uses encryption, access controls, and audit trails to protect sensitive information and maintain the integrity of the data throughout the eDiscovery process.

119. What is the role of Microsoft Information Protection in Microsoft Purview?

Microsoft Information Protection in Microsoft Purview provides tools to discover, classify, and protect sensitive information across an organization. It integrates with sensitivity labels, DLP policies, and encryption to ensure that data is consistently protected, regardless of where it is stored or used.

120. How does Microsoft Purview help organizations manage regulatory changes?

Microsoft Purview helps organizations manage regulatory changes by providing continuous updates to compliance templates and controls. It offers insights into new and evolving regulations, helping organizations adapt their compliance strategies and ensure ongoing adherence to regulatory requirements.

Multiple Choice Questions

Describe the Concepts of Security, Compliance, and Identity

1. What is the primary purpose of multi-factor authentication (MFA)?

> A) To provide a single sign-on experience
> B) To improve password complexity
> C) To enhance security by requiring multiple forms of verification
> D) To reduce the number of passwords a user must remember

Correct Answer: C) To enhance security by requiring multiple forms of verification.

Explanation: Multi-factor authentication (MFA) adds an extra layer of security by requiring users to provide two or more verification methods before gaining access. This significantly reduces the risk of unauthorized access, even if passwords are compromised.

2. What is the principle of least privilege?

> A) Granting the minimum permissions necessary to perform a task
> B) Giving all users full access to all systems

C) Providing administrative privileges to trusted users

D) Assigning privileges based on user preference

Correct Answer: A) Granting the minimum permissions necessary to perform a task.

Explanation: The principle of least privilege involves granting users only the permissions they need to perform their tasks, minimizing potential security risks. This helps reduce the attack surface and prevent misuse of privileges.

3. What is the purpose of a security information and event management (SIEM) system?

A) To store large amounts of data

B) To automate software updates

C) To provide real-time analysis of security alerts

D) To manage user identities

Correct Answer: C) To provide real-time analysis of security alerts.

Explanation: A SIEM system collects and analyzes security event data from various sources in real-time to detect, analyze, and respond to potential security threats. This is crucial for maintaining a secure environment and ensuring timely responses to incidents.

4. What is data encryption at rest?

A) Encrypting data while it is being transmitted
B) Encrypting data when it is stored on disk
C) Encrypting data during processing
D) Encrypting data in the cloud

Correct Answer: B) Encrypting data when it is stored on disk.

Explanation: Data encryption at rest ensures that data stored on disk is encrypted, protecting it from unauthorized access and ensuring data confidentiality. This is important for compliance with data protection regulations and safeguarding sensitive information.

5. What is an identity provider (IdP)?

A) A service that manages user identities and authentication
B) A tool for managing network security
C) A type of firewall
D) A cloud storage solution

Correct Answer: A) A service that manages user identities and authentication.

Explanation: An identity provider (IdP) is responsible for authenticating users and managing their identities. This is critical for enabling secure access to resources and ensuring that only authorized users can access sensitive information.

6. Which of the following is a key benefit of single sign-on (SSO)?

A) Reduced need for multi-factor authentication
B) Improved security through password complexity
C) Simplified user access management
D) Increased use of local storage

Correct Answer: C) Simplified user access management

Explanation: Single sign-on (SSO) allows users to access multiple applications with a single set of credentials, simplifying access management and improving user experience. It also reduces the number of passwords users need to remember, enhancing security.

7. What is a compliance audit?

A) A tool for monitoring network traffic
B) An evaluation of an organization's adherence to regulatory requirements
C) A method for encrypting data
D) A process for managing user identities

Correct Answer: B) An evaluation of an organization's adherence to regulatory requirements.

Explanation: A compliance audit assesses an organization's compliance with regulatory requirements and industry standards. It is important for ensuring that the organization meets legal obligations and avoids penalties.

8. What does the acronym GDPR stand for?

A) General Data Protection Regulation
B) General Data Policy Review
C) Global Data Privacy Regulation
D) General Digital Privacy Regulation

Correct Answer: A) General Data Protection Regulation

Explanation: The General Data Protection Regulation (GDPR) is a regulation that mandates data protection and privacy for individuals within the European Union. It is crucial for organizations to comply with GDPR to protect personal data and avoid hefty fines.

9. What is the role of a data protection officer (DPO)?

A) To manage network security
B) To oversee an organization's data protection strategy and compliance
C) To develop software applications
D) To maintain physical security of data centers

Correct Answer: B) To oversee an organization's data protection strategy and compliance.

Explanation: A data protection officer (DPO) is responsible for ensuring that an organization complies with data protection laws and implements effective data protection strategies. This role is crucial for safeguarding personal data and maintaining regulatory compliance.

10. What is the primary goal of zero trust security?

A) To allow unrestricted access to all users
B) To provide a single layer of security
C) To verify and secure every access request, regardless of its origin
D) To minimize the use of encryption

Correct Answer: C) To verify and secure every access request, regardless of its origin.

Explanation: Zero trust security is based on the principle of "never trust, always verify," ensuring that every access request is authenticated and authorized, regardless of whether it comes from inside or outside the network. This approach reduces the risk of security breaches.

11. What is a security incident response plan?

A) A plan for developing software applications
B) A strategy for responding to and managing security incidents
C) A method for encrypting data
D) A process for managing network traffic

Correct Answer: B) A strategy for responding to and managing security incidents.

Explanation: A security incident response plan outlines the steps an organization should take to detect, respond to, and recover from security incidents. Having an effective incident response plan is critical for minimizing the impact of security breaches and ensuring business continuity.

12. What is a security policy?

A) A set of rules and practices that specify how an organization protects its information assets

B) A tool for monitoring application performance

C) A method for managing user identities

D) A service for hosting web applications

Correct Answer: A) A set of rules and practices that specify how an organization protects its information assets.

Explanation: A security policy is a formal document that defines how an organization protects its information assets. It provides guidelines for employees and outlines the measures to be taken to ensure information security, helping to prevent unauthorized access and data breaches.

13. What is the main purpose of a firewall?

A) To store large amounts of data

B) To manage user identities

C) To monitor network traffic and block unauthorized access

D) To develop software applications

Correct Answer: C) To monitor network traffic and block unauthorized access.

Explanation: A firewall is a network security device that monitors and controls incoming and outgoing network traffic based on predetermined security rules. Its main purpose is to block unauthorized access and protect the network from security threats.

14. What is the function of an intrusion detection system (IDS)?

A) To encrypt data at rest

B) To detect and alert on potential security breaches

C) To manage user access

D) To store backup data

Correct Answer: B) To detect and alert on potential security breaches.

Explanation: An intrusion detection system (IDS) monitors network traffic for suspicious activity and potential security breaches, generating alerts for further investigation. It is important for identifying and responding to threats in real time.

15. What is data masking?

A) A method for encrypting data
B) A technique for obscuring sensitive data to protect it from unauthorized access
C) A tool for managing network security
D) A process for developing software applications

Correct Answer: B) A technique for obscuring sensitive data to protect it from unauthorized access.

Explanation: Data masking involves creating a similar but inauthentic version of data that can be used for testing and development without exposing sensitive information. This helps protect sensitive data from unauthorized access while maintaining its usability.

16. What is the purpose of a vulnerability assessment?

A) To develop new software applications
B) To identify and evaluate security weaknesses in a system
C) To manage network traffic
D) To encrypt data in transit

Correct Answer: B) To identify and evaluate security weaknesses in a system.

Explanation: A vulnerability assessment involves identifying, quantifying, and prioritizing vulnerabilities in a system. This helps organizations understand their security posture and take necessary steps to mitigate risks.

17. What does the term 'phishing' refer to?

A) A technique for encrypting data
B) A method for developing software
C) A type of cyber attack that uses deceptive emails to steal sensitive information
D) A process for managing network security

Correct Answer: C) A type of cyber attack that uses deceptive emails to steal sensitive information.

Explanation: Phishing is a cyber attack in which attackers use deceptive emails to trick recipients into revealing sensitive information, such as passwords and credit card numbers. Awareness and training are important for preventing phishing attacks.

18. What is the importance of security awareness training?

A) To develop software applications
B) To educate employees on security best practices and reduce the risk of human error
C) To manage network traffic
D) To encrypt data at rest

Correct Answer: B) To educate employees on security best practices and reduce the risk of human error.

Explanation: Security awareness training educates employees about security threats and best practices, helping to reduce the risk of human error and improve overall security posture. It is essential for creating a security-conscious culture within the organization.

19. What is the role of encryption in data security?

A) To increase data storage capacity

B) To protect data by converting it into an unreadable format

C) To manage user access

D) To develop software applications

Correct Answer: B) To protect data by converting it into an unreadable format.

Explanation: Encryption protects data by converting it into an unreadable format that can only be decrypted by authorized parties. This ensures the confidentiality and integrity of data, both at rest and in transit.

20. What is a security breach?

A) A successful attempt to access, use, or disclose data without authorization

B) A method for encrypting data

C) A process for managing network security

D) A tool for monitoring application performance

Correct Answer: A) A successful attempt to access, use, or disclose data without authorization.

Explanation: A security breach occurs when an unauthorized party gains access to data, systems, or networks. It can result in data loss, financial loss, and damage to an organization's reputation. Preventing and responding to security breaches is crucial for maintaining security.

21. What is the purpose of a security operations center (SOC)?

A) To develop software applications
B) To manage user identities
C) To monitor and respond to security incidents in real-time
D) To store large amounts of data

Correct Answer: C) To monitor and respond to security incidents in real-time.

Explanation: A security operations center (SOC) is a centralized unit that monitors and responds to security incidents in real-time. The SOC is essential for maintaining situational awareness and ensuring a timely response to security threats.

22. What is the significance of the CIA triad in information security?

A) To develop software applications

B) To ensure the Confidentiality, Integrity, and Availability of information

C) To manage network traffic

D) To encrypt data at rest

Correct Answer: B) To ensure the Confidentiality, Integrity, and Availability of information.

Explanation: The CIA triad is a fundamental concept in information security that stands for Confidentiality, Integrity, and Availability. It ensures that information is protected from unauthorized access (confidentiality), remains accurate and unaltered (integrity), and is accessible when needed (availability).

23. What is the purpose of access control?

A) To develop software applications

B) To manage network traffic

C) To restrict access to information and systems to authorized users only

D) To store large amounts of data

Correct Answer: C) To restrict access to information and systems to authorized users only.

Explanation: Access control involves restricting access to information and systems to authorized users only, ensuring that sensitive data is protected from unauthorized access and misuse. Implementing effective access control measures is critical for maintaining security.

24. What is a digital certificate?

A) A tool for encrypting data
B) An electronic document that verifies the identity of a user or device
C) A method for developing software
D) A process for managing network security

Correct Answer: B) An electronic document that verifies the identity of a user or device.

Explanation: A digital certificate is an electronic document that verifies the identity of a user or device, enabling secure communication and authentication. It is issued by a trusted certificate authority (CA) and contains information such as the certificate holder's public key and digital signature.

25. What is two-factor authentication (2FA)?

A) A method for encrypting data
B) A security process that requires two forms of verification
C) A tool for managing network traffic
D) A process for developing software applications

Correct Answer: B) A security process that requires two forms of verification.

Explanation: Two-factor authentication (2FA) is a security process that requires users to provide two forms of verification, typically something they know (e.g., password) and something they have (e.g., a mobile device). This enhances security by adding an extra layer of protection against unauthorized access.

Describe the Capabilities of Microsoft Identity and Access Management Solutions:

1. What is the primary function of Azure Active Directory (Azure AD)?

> A) To store large amounts of data
> B) To manage user identities and access to resources
> C) To develop software applications
> D) To monitor network traffic

Correct Answer: B) To manage user identities and access to resources.

Explanation: Azure Active Directory (Azure AD) is a cloud-based identity and access management service that provides authentication and authorization for users and applications. It helps organizations manage user identities, enforce access policies, and enable single sign-on (SSO).

2. What is the purpose of role-based access control (RBAC) in Azure AD?

> A) To encrypt data at rest

B) To assign permissions to users based on their roles

C) To develop software applications

D) To manage network traffic

Correct Answer: B) To assign permissions to users based on their roles.

Explanation: Role-based access control (RBAC) in Azure AD allows organizations to assign permissions to users based on their roles, ensuring that users have the appropriate level of access to resources. This helps enforce the principle of least privilege and improves security.

3. What is Azure AD Conditional Access?

A) A service that enforces access policies based on specific conditions

B) A tool for monitoring application performance

C) A method for developing software

D) A process for encrypting data

Correct Answer: A) A service that enforces access policies based on specific conditions.

Explanation: Azure AD Conditional Access allows organizations to define and enforce access policies based on specific conditions, such as user location, device state, and risk level. This helps ensure secure access to resources and reduces the risk of unauthorized access.

4. What is the benefit of single sign-on (SSO) with Azure AD?

        A) Increased use of local storage
        B) Reduced need for multi-factor authentication
        C) Improved password complexity
        D) Simplified user access to multiple applications with one set of credentials

Correct Answer: D) Simplified user access to multiple applications with one set of credentials.

Explanation: Single sign-on (SSO) with Azure AD allows users to access multiple applications with a single set of credentials, simplifying access management and improving user experience. This reduces the number of passwords users need to remember and enhances security.

5. What is Azure AD Privileged Identity Management (PIM)?

        A) A service for storing large amounts of data
        B) A tool for managing network security
        C) A service that helps manage, control, and monitor access to important resources
        D) A method for developing software

Correct Answer: C) A service that helps manage, control, and monitor access to important resources.

Explanation: Azure AD Privileged Identity Management (PIM) is a service that helps organizations manage, control, and monitor access to important resources. It provides just-in-time access, approval workflows, and activity logging to enhance security and reduce the risk of privilege abuse.

6. What is the function of Azure AD Identity Protection?

A) To store backup data

B) To manage user access

C) To detect and respond to identity-based risks

D) To develop software applications

Correct Answer: C) To detect and respond to identity-based risks.

Explanation: Azure AD Identity Protection helps organizations detect and respond to identity-based risks, such as compromised accounts and suspicious sign-in activities. It uses machine learning and behavioral analytics to identify potential threats and take appropriate actions.

7. What is Azure AD B2C (Business to Consumer)?

A) A service for monitoring application performance

B) A tool for managing network traffic

C) A service that enables businesses to provide identity and access management to their customers

D) A method for encrypting data

Correct Answer: C) A service that enables businesses to provide identity and access management to their customers.

Explanation: Azure AD B2C (Business to Consumer) is a cloud-based identity and access management service that allows businesses to provide authentication and authorization for their customers. It supports custom branding and integration with various identity providers, enhancing user experience.

8. What is the purpose of Azure AD Application Proxy?

      A) To encrypt data in transit
      B) To develop software applications
      C) To manage user identities
      D) To provide secure remote access to on-premises applications

Correct Answer: D) To provide secure remote access to on-premises applications.

Explanation: Azure AD Application Proxy enables secure remote access to on-premises applications by acting as a reverse proxy. It allows users to access internal applications from outside the corporate network without the need for a VPN, improving security and accessibility.

9. What is the significance of user and group management in Azure AD?

A) To increase data storage capacity

B) To manage user identities and group memberships, ensuring appropriate access to resources

C) To manage user identities

D) To develop software applications

Correct Answer: B) To manage user identities and group memberships, ensuring appropriate access to resources.

Explanation: User and group management in Azure AD involves managing user identities and group memberships, which helps ensure that users have appropriate access to resources. This is crucial for maintaining security and enforcing access policies.

10. What is Azure AD Connect?

A) A tool for synchronizing on-premises directories with Azure AD

B) A service for developing software applications

C) A tool for encrypting data

D) A process for managing network security

Correct Answer: A) A tool for synchronizing on-premises directories with Azure AD.

Explanation: Azure AD Connect is a tool that synchronizes on-premises directories, such as Windows Server Active Directory, with Azure AD. This allows organizations to maintain a consistent identity across on-premises and cloud environments, simplifying identity management.

11. What is the purpose of self-service password reset (SSPR) in Azure AD?

> A) To allow users to reset their passwords without administrator intervention
> B) To manage network traffic
> C) To increase data storage capacity
> D) To develop software applications

Correct Answer: A) To allow users to reset their passwords without administrator intervention.

Explanation: Self-service password reset (SSPR) in Azure AD enables users to reset their passwords without needing assistance from administrators. This reduces the burden on IT support and improves user productivity by allowing users to quickly regain access to their accounts.

12. What is Azure AD Domain Services?

> A) A managed domain service that provides domain join, group policy, and LDAP capabilities
> B) A tool for managing network traffic
> C) A service for monitoring application performance
> D) A method for encrypting data

Correct Answer: A) A managed domain service that provides domain join, group policy, and LDAP capabilities.

Explanation: Azure AD Domain Services is a managed domain service that provides traditional Active Directory features, such as domain join, group policy, and LDAP, in the Azure cloud. This allows organizations to use familiar Active Directory capabilities without managing on-premises infrastructure.

13. What is the function of Azure AD Conditional Access policies?

A) To increase data storage capacity
B) To monitor application performance
C) To enforce access controls based on conditions such as user location and device state
D) To develop software applications

Correct Answer: C) To enforce access controls based on conditions such as user location and device state.

Explanation: Azure AD Conditional Access policies allow organizations to enforce access controls based on specific conditions, such as user location, device state, and risk level. This helps ensure secure access to resources and reduces the risk of unauthorized access.

14. What is the purpose of Azure AD Multi-Factor Authentication (MFA)?

A) To increase data storage capacity
B) To enhance security by requiring multiple forms of verification during sign-in
C) To develop software applications
D) To manage network traffic

Correct Answer: B) To enhance security by requiring multiple forms of verification during sign-in.

Explanation: Azure AD Multi-Factor Authentication (MFA) enhances security by requiring users to provide multiple forms of verification during sign-in, such as a password and a one-time code sent to their mobile device. This reduces the risk of unauthorized access and improves overall security.

15. What is the role of Azure AD B2B (Business to Business)?

A) To store large amounts of data
B) To monitor application performance
C) To enable secure collaboration between organizations by providing guest access
D) To develop software applications

Correct Answer: C) To enable secure collaboration between organizations by providing guest access.

Explanation: Azure AD B2B (Business to Business) allows organizations to collaborate securely with external partners by providing guest access to their resources. This facilitates collaboration while maintaining control over access and security.

16. What is Azure AD Identity Governance?

A) A set of capabilities that help organizations manage and secure identities
B) A service for managing network traffic
C) A tool for encrypting data
D) A method for developing software applications

Correct Answer: A) A set of capabilities that help organizations manage and secure identities.

Explanation: Azure AD Identity Governance provides a set of capabilities that help organizations manage and secure identities, ensuring that users have the right access to the right resources. This includes features like access reviews, entitlement management, and privileged identity management.

17. What is the purpose of Azure AD Access Reviews?

A) To increase data storage capacity
B) To periodically review and certify user access to resources
C) To manage network traffic
D) To develop software applications

Correct Answer: B) To periodically review and certify user access to resources.

Explanation: Azure AD Access Reviews allow organizations to periodically review and certify user access to resources, ensuring that only authorized users have access. This helps maintain security and compliance by identifying and removing unnecessary access.

18. What is the function of Azure AD Application Proxy?

A) To encrypt data at rest
B) To develop software applications
C) To provide secure remote access to on-premises applications
D) To manage user identities

Correct Answer: C) To provide secure remote access to on-premises applications.

Explanation: Azure AD Application Proxy enables secure remote access to on-premises applications by acting as a reverse proxy. It allows users to access internal applications from outside the corporate network without the need for a VPN, improving security and accessibility.

19. What is the significance of user and group management in Azure AD?

A) To increase data storage capacity
B) To manage user identities and group memberships, ensuring appropriate access to resources

C) To improve application performance

D) To develop software applications

Correct Answer: B) To manage user identities and group memberships, ensuring appropriate access to resources.

Explanation: User and group management in Azure AD involves managing user identities and group memberships, which helps ensure that users have appropriate access to resources. This is crucial for maintaining security and enforcing access policies.

20. What is Azure AD Connect?

A) A tool for encrypting data

B) A service for developing software applications

C) A tool for synchronizing on-premises directories with Azure AD

D) A process for managing network security

Correct Answer: C) A tool for synchronizing on-premises directories with Azure AD.

Explanation: Azure AD Connect is a tool that synchronizes on-premises directories, such as Windows Server Active Directory, with Azure AD. This allows organizations to maintain a consistent identity across on-premises and cloud environments, simplifying identity management.

21. What is the purpose of self-service password reset (SSPR) in Azure AD?

A) To increase data storage capacity

B) To allow users to reset their passwords without administrator intervention

C) To manage network traffic

D) To develop software applications

Correct Answer: B) To allow users to reset their passwords without administrator intervention.

Explanation: Self-service password reset (SSPR) in Azure AD enables users to reset their passwords without needing assistance from administrators. This reduces the burden on IT support and improves user productivity by allowing users to quickly regain access to their accounts.

22. What is Azure AD Domain Services?

A) A service for monitoring application performance

B) A tool for managing network traffic

C) A managed domain service that provides domain join, group policy, and LDAP capabilities

D) A method for encrypting data

Correct Answer: C) A managed domain service that provides domain join, group policy, and LDAP capabilities.

Explanation: Azure AD Domain Services is a managed domain service that provides traditional Active Directory features, such as domain join, group policy, and LDAP, in the Azure cloud. This allows organizations to use familiar Active Directory capabilities without managing on-premises infrastructure.

23. What is the function of Azure AD Conditional Access policies?

      A) To increase data storage capacity

      B) To monitor application performance

      C) To enforce access controls based on conditions such as user location and device state

      D) To develop software applications

Correct Answer: C) To enforce access controls based on conditions such as user location and device state.

Explanation: Azure AD Conditional Access policies allow organizations to enforce access controls based on specific conditions, such as user location, device state, and risk level. This helps ensure secure access to resources and reduces the risk of unauthorized access.

24. What is the purpose of Azure AD Multi-Factor Authentication (MFA)?

      A) To increase data storage capacity

      B) To develop software applications

      C) To store large amounts of data

D) To enhance security by requiring multiple forms of verification during sign-in

Correct Answer: D) To enhance security by requiring multiple forms of verification during sign-in.

Explanation: Azure AD Multi-Factor Authentication (MFA) enhances security by requiring users to provide multiple forms of verification during sign-in, such as a password and a one-time code sent to their mobile device. This reduces the risk of unauthorized access and improves overall security.

25. What is the role of Azure AD B2B (Business to Business)?

A) To enable secure collaboration between organizations by providing guest access
B) To monitor application performance
C) A method for encrypting data
D) To develop software applications

Correct Answer: A) To enable secure collaboration between organizations by providing guest access.

Explanation: Azure AD B2B (Business to Business) allows organizations to collaborate securely with external partners by providing guest access to their resources. This facilitates collaboration while maintaining control over access and security.

Describe the Capabilities of Microsoft Security Solutions:

1. What is the purpose of Microsoft Defender for Cloud?

A) To provide cloud storage solutions
B) To offer advanced threat protection and unified security management across hybrid environments
C) To manage network traffic and load balancing
D) To provide identity management services

Answer: B
Explanation: Microsoft Defender for Cloud provides advanced threat protection and unified security management across hybrid cloud environments, continuously assessing security posture and protecting workloads from evolving threats.

2. How does Azure Security Center help in managing security across hybrid workloads?

A) By offering continuous security assessment, threat protection, and unified security management
B) By providing identity verification
C) By managing cloud storage and backups
D) By providing customer relationship management

Answer: A) By offering continuous security assessment, threat protection, and unified security management.

Explanation: Azure Security Center strengthens the security posture of data centers by providing continuous security assessment, threat protection, and unified security management across both Azure and on-premises resources.

3. What are the key features of Microsoft Sentinel?

A) Data storage and backup
B) Email marketing and automation
C) Network traffic management
D) Intelligent security analytics, threat intelligence, and automated incident response

Answer: D) Intelligent security analytics, threat intelligence, and automated incident response

Explanation: Microsoft Sentinel offers intelligent security analytics and threat intelligence, utilizing AI and machine learning to detect and respond to threats, automate incident response, and provide comprehensive visibility across the organization.

4. How does Microsoft Defender for Endpoint enhance endpoint security?

A) By offering endpoint detection and response (EDR), automated investigation, and threat intelligence integration

B) By providing cloud storage solutions
C) By managing customer data
D) By providing email marketing tools

Answer: A) By offering endpoint detection and response (EDR), automated investigation, and threat intelligence integration.

Explanation: Microsoft Defender for Endpoint provides advanced endpoint detection and response (EDR), automated investigation and remediation, and integrates threat intelligence to prevent, detect, and respond to advanced threats.

5. What is the function of Azure DDoS Protection?

A) To safeguard applications from Distributed Denial-of-Service attacks
B) To provide identity management
C) To manage cloud storage
D) To provide email marketing services

Answer: A) To safeguard applications from Distributed Denial-of-Service attacks.

Explanation: Azure DDoS Protection safeguards applications from Distributed Denial-of-Service attacks by continuously monitoring incoming traffic, automatically applying mitigation strategies, and providing detailed attack metrics and reports.

6. Explain the role of Azure Firewall in network security.

A) To manage customer relationships
B) To manage cloud storage
C) To provide email automation
D) To control inbound and outbound traffic using rules and policies

Answer: D) To control inbound and outbound traffic using rules and policies

Explanation: Azure Firewall is a managed network security service that controls inbound and outbound traffic using rules and policies, integrates with threat intelligence, and provides high availability and scalability.

7. What capabilities does Microsoft Defender for Identity provide?

A) Email marketing automation
B) Cloud storage management
C) Identity-based threat protection using behavioral analytics
D) Customer relationship management

Answer: C) Identity-based threat protection using behavioral analytics.

Explanation: Microsoft Defender for Identity helps protect on-premises Active Directory from identity-based threats by using behavioral analytics to detect suspicious activities, compromised accounts, and lateral movement within the network.

8. How does Microsoft Cloud App Security enhance cloud application security?

A) By offering visibility and control over cloud applications, threat detection, and data protection policies

B) By providing email marketing tools

C) By managing network traffic

D) By providing identity verification

Answer: A) By offering visibility and control over cloud applications, threat detection, and data protection policies

Explanation: Microsoft Cloud App Security provides visibility and control over cloud applications, detects and responds to threats, enforces data protection policies, and manages application usage to ensure security and compliance.

9. Describe the importance of Azure Key Vault in securing sensitive information.

A) To provide customer support services

B) To securely store and manage cryptographic keys, secrets, and certificates

C) To manage email marketing

D) To offer network traffic management

Answer: B) To securely store and manage cryptographic keys, secrets, and certificates.

Explanation: Azure Key Vault securely stores and manages cryptographic keys, secrets, and certificates, providing centralized management, access control, and logging to protect sensitive data and ensure secure key management practices.

10. How does Microsoft Defender for Office 365 protect against email threats?

      A) By offering advanced threat protection, safe links and attachments, and anti-phishing policies
      B) By providing cloud storage
      C) By managing network traffic
      D) By providing customer relationship management

Answer: A) By offering advanced threat protection, safe links and attachments, and anti-phishing policies.

Explanation: Microsoft Defender for Office 365 protects against email-based threats like phishing, malware, and spam by providing advanced threat protection, safe links and attachments, and anti-phishing policies.

11. What is the purpose of Microsoft Defender Vulnerability Management?

A) To manage customer data
B) To identify and mitigate vulnerabilities across endpoints
C) To provide email marketing automation
D) To manage cloud storage

Answer: B) To identify and mitigate vulnerabilities across endpoints

Explanation: Microsoft Defender Vulnerability Management identifies and mitigates vulnerabilities across endpoints, continuously assessing and prioritizing vulnerabilities and providing remediation recommendations to reduce risks.

12. How does Azure Sentinel utilize machine learning to enhance security?

A) By managing cloud storage
B) By managing customer relationships
C) By providing email automation
D) By using machine learning to analyze security data, detect anomalies, and identify potential threats

Answer: D) By using machine learning to analyze security data, detect anomalies, and identify potential threats.

Explanation: Azure Sentinel uses machine learning to analyze security data, detect anomalies, identify potential threats, and provide advanced analytics and automated threat detection to improve security operations.

13. Explain the role of threat hunting in Microsoft security solutions.

A) To manage email marketing
B) To proactively search for hidden threats and vulnerabilities within an organization's environment
C) To provide cloud storage solutions
D) To manage customer relationships

Answer: B) To proactively search for hidden threats and vulnerabilities within an organization's environment.

Explanation: Threat hunting involves proactively searching for hidden threats and vulnerabilities within an organization's environment using Microsoft security tools, enabling security teams to identify and mitigate potential threats before they can cause harm.

14. How does Microsoft Defender for Cloud Apps enforce data protection policies?

A) By managing customer data
B) By providing email marketing tools
C) By monitoring and controlling data transfers, applying encryption, and preventing unauthorized access
D) By managing cloud storage

Answer: C) By monitoring and controlling data transfers, applying encryption, and preventing unauthorized access.

Explanation: Microsoft Defender for Cloud Apps enforces data protection policies by monitoring and controlling data transfers, applying encryption, and preventing unauthorized access to ensure data security and compliance.

15. What are the benefits of using Azure Security Center for compliance management?

A) To manage customer relationships
B) To manage email marketing automation
C) To monitor security posture, identify compliance violations, and provide tools to ensure adherence to regulatory standards
D) To provide cloud storage solutions

Answer: C) To monitor security posture, identify compliance violations, and provide tools to ensure adherence to regulatory standards.

Explanation: Azure Security Center helps organizations manage compliance by continuously monitoring security posture, identifying compliance violations, and providing tools to ensure adherence to regulatory standards and organizational policies.

16. Describe the concept of endpoint detection and response (EDR) in Microsoft Defender.

A) To provide email marketing
B) To continuously monitor and analyze

endpoint activities to detect and respond to advanced threats

C) To manage customer data

D) To provide cloud storage solutions

Answer: B) To continuously monitor and analyze endpoint activities to detect and respond to advanced threats.

Explanation: EDR in Microsoft Defender involves continuous monitoring and analysis of endpoint activities to detect and respond to advanced threats, using behavioral analytics and threat intelligence to identify suspicious patterns and mitigate security incidents.

17. How does Microsoft Defender for Identity protect against lateral movement attacks?

A) By detecting suspicious activities and abnormal access patterns using advanced analytics

B) By managing cloud storage

C) By providing email marketing automation

D) By managing customer relationships

Answer: A) By detecting suspicious activities and abnormal access patterns using advanced analytics.

Explanation: Microsoft Defender for Identity uses advanced analytics to detect suspicious activities and abnormal access patterns, providing alerts and detailed reports to help security teams investigate and respond to potential lateral movement attacks.

18. What capabilities does Microsoft Cloud Security Posture Management (CSPM) provide?

A) To manage customer data
B) To manage network traffic
C) To provide email marketing tools
D) To continuously monitor, identify, and remediate security risks in cloud environments

Answer: D) To continuously monitor, identify, and remediate security risks in cloud environments

Explanation: Microsoft CSPM helps organizations manage and improve their cloud security posture by continuously monitoring, identifying, and remediating security risks, providing visibility into misconfigurations and compliance violations.

19. How does Microsoft Defender for Endpoint integrate with other Microsoft security solutions?

A) By managing cloud storage
B) By integrating with solutions like Microsoft Defender for Office 365 and Azure Security Center for a unified approach to threat detection and response
C) By providing email marketing automation
D) By managing customer relationships

Answer: B) By integrating with solutions like Microsoft Defender for Office 365 and Azure Security Center for a unified approach to threat detection and response.

Explanation: Microsoft Defender for Endpoint integrates with solutions like Microsoft Defender for Office 365, Azure Security Center, and Microsoft Cloud App Security, providing a unified approach to threat detection, investigation, and response across endpoints and cloud environments.

20. Explain the significance of automated threat response in Microsoft security solutions.

A) To manage email marketing
B) To detect, investigate, and respond to security incidents automatically, reducing mitigation time and human error
C) To provide cloud storage solutions
D) To manage customer relationships

Answer: B) To detect, investigate, and respond to security incidents automatically, reducing mitigation time and human error.

Explanation: Automated threat response uses machine learning and automation to detect, investigate, and respond to security incidents, reducing the time to mitigate threats, minimizing human error, and ensuring timely and consistent incident handling.

21. What is the role of threat intelligence in Microsoft security solutions?

A) To collect and analyze data on emerging threats, enhancing detection capabilities and informing security policies
B) To provide email marketing automation
C) To manage cloud storage
D) To manage customer relationships

Answer: A) To collect and analyze data on emerging threats, enhancing detection capabilities and informing security policies.

Explanation: Threat intelligence in Microsoft security solutions involves collecting and analyzing data on emerging threats, enhancing detection capabilities, informing security policies

18. What capabilities does Microsoft Cloud Security Posture Management (CSPM) provide?

A) To manage customer data
B) To provide email marketing tools
C) To continuously monitor, identify, and remediate security risks in cloud environments
D) To manage network traffic

Answer: C)To continuously monitor, identify, and remediate security risks in cloud environments.

Explanation: Microsoft CSPM helps organizations manage and improve their cloud security posture by continuously monitoring, identifying, and remediating security risks, providing visibility into misconfigurations and compliance violations.

23. How does Microsoft Defender for Cloud Apps enhance data protection?

A) By managing customer relationships
B) By monitoring and controlling data transfers, applying encryption, and preventing unauthorized access
C) By providing email marketing tools
D) By managing cloud storage

Answer: B) By monitoring and controlling data transfers, applying encryption, and preventing.

Explanation: Microsoft Defender for Cloud Apps enhances data protection by monitoring and controlling data transfers, applying encryption, and preventing unauthorized access, ensuring that sensitive information is securely managed.

24. What is the significance of Azure Security Center in improving security posture?

A) To provide cloud storage solutions
B) To offer email marketing tools
C) To manage customer relationships
D) To continuously monitor security posture, identify vulnerabilities, and provide recommendations for improvement

Answer: D) To continuously monitor security posture, identify vulnerabilities, and provide.

Explanation: The significance of Azure Security Center

in improving security posture lies in its ability to continuously monitor security posture, identify vulnerabilities, and provide actionable recommendations for improvement, helping organizations maintain a robust security environment.

25. How does Microsoft Defender for Endpoint handle automated investigation and remediation?

A) By managing email marketing campaigns
B) By using automated tools to investigate and remediate security threats, reducing the burden on IT teams
C) By providing cloud storage solutions
D) By managing customer relationships

Answer: B) By using automated tools to investigate and remediate security threats, reducing the burden on IT teams

Explanation: Microsoft Defender for Endpoint handles automated investigation and remediation by using automated tools to investigate and remediate security threats, reducing the burden on IT teams and ensuring timely response to security incidents.

Describe the Capabilities of Microsoft Compliance Solutions:

1. What is Microsoft Compliance Manager?

A) A tool for monitoring network traffic
B) A service for managing user identities
C) A workflow-based tool that helps manage compliance activities
D) A method for encrypting data

Correct Answer: C) A workflow-based tool that helps manage compliance activities.

Explanation: Microsoft Compliance Manager is a workflow-based tool that helps organizations manage compliance activities, track regulatory requirements, and implement best practices. It provides a compliance score and actionable insights to improve compliance posture.

2. What is the purpose of Microsoft Information Governance?

A) To store large amounts of data
B) To develop software applications
C) To help organizations manage and govern their information lifecycle
D) To manage network traffic

Correct Answer: C) To help organizations manage and govern their information lifecycle.

Explanation: Microsoft Information Governance provides tools and capabilities to help organizations manage and govern their information lifecycle, from creation to disposal. It helps ensure that information is retained, protected, and disposed of according to compliance requirements.

3. What is Microsoft Insider Risk Management?

A) A tool for encrypting data at rest

B) A solution that helps detect and mitigate insider risks

C) A service for monitoring application performance

D) A method for developing software applications

Correct Answer: B) A solution that helps detect and mitigate insider risks.

Explanation: Microsoft Insider Risk Management helps organizations detect and mitigate insider risks, such as data leaks, intellectual property theft, and other malicious activities. It uses machine learning and behavioral analytics to identify potential risks and take appropriate actions.

4. What is the function of Microsoft Information Protection (MIP)?

A) To increase data storage capacity

B) To manage network traffic

C) To classify, label, and protect sensitive information

D) To develop software applications

Correct Answer: C) To classify, label, and protect sensitive information.

Explanation: Microsoft Information Protection (MIP) helps organizations classify, label, and protect sensitive information based on its sensitivity. It provides tools for applying protection policies, tracking data usage, and ensuring compliance with data protection regulations.

5. What is the purpose of Microsoft Compliance Score?

A) To store large amounts of data

B) To develop software applications

C) To provide a measure of an organization's compliance posture

D) To manage network traffic

Correct Answer: C) To provide a measure of an organization's compliance posture.

Explanation: Microsoft Compliance Score provides a measure of an organization's compliance posture by assessing its compliance with regulatory requirements and best practices. It offers actionable insights to help improve compliance and reduce risks.

6. What is Microsoft Data Loss Prevention (DLP)?

A) A tool for encrypting data at rest

B) A service for monitoring application performance

C) A solution that helps prevent the accidental sharing of sensitive information

D) A method for developing software applications

Correct Answer: C) A solution that helps prevent the accidental sharing of sensitive information.

Explanation: Microsoft Data Loss Prevention (DLP) helps prevent the accidental sharing of sensitive information by identifying, monitoring, and protecting sensitive data. It enforces policies to prevent data leaks and ensures compliance with data protection regulations.

7. What is the role of Microsoft eDiscovery?

A) To store large amounts of data

B) To help organizations identify, collect, and review electronic information for legal and compliance purposes

C) To increase data storage capacity

D) To manage network traffic

Correct Answer: B) To help organizations identify, collect, and review electronic information for legal and compliance purposes.

Explanation: Microsoft eDiscovery helps organizations identify, collect, and review electronic information for legal and compliance purposes. It provides tools for searching and analyzing data across various sources, ensuring that relevant information is available for legal proceedings.

8. What is the function of Microsoft Compliance Manager assessments?

A) To increase data storage capacity

B) To manage network traffic

C) To assess an organization's compliance with specific regulations and standards

D) To develop software applications

Correct Answer: C) To assess an organization's compliance with specific regulations and standards.

Explanation: Microsoft Compliance Manager assessments evaluate an organization's compliance with specific regulations and standards, such as GDPR and ISO 27001. They provide a compliance score and actionable insights to help improve compliance and reduce risks.

9. What is the purpose of Microsoft Advanced Audit?

A) To store large amounts of data

B) To monitor application performance

C) To provide enhanced auditing capabilities for security and compliance

D) To develop software applications

Correct Answer: C) To provide enhanced auditing capabilities for security and compliance.

Explanation: Microsoft Advanced Audit provides enhanced auditing capabilities for security and compliance, allowing organizations to retain audit logs for longer periods and access critical events. This helps ensure that organizations can meet regulatory requirements and investigate potential security incidents.

10. What is Microsoft Compliance Manager's compliance score?

A) A tool for encrypting data at rest
B) A measure of an organization's compliance posture based on assessments
C) A service for managing network traffic
D) A method for developing software applications

Correct Answer: B) A measure of an organization's compliance posture based on assessments.

Explanation: Microsoft Compliance Manager's compliance score is a measure of an organization's compliance posture based on assessments of its compliance with specific regulations and standards. It provides actionable insights to help improve compliance and reduce risks.

11. What is the role of Microsoft Priva?

A) To store large amounts of data

B) To develop software applications

C) To develop software applications

D) To help organizations manage and protect personal data

Correct Answer: D) To help organizations manage and protect personal data.

Explanation: Microsoft Priva helps organizations manage and protect personal data, ensuring compliance with data protection regulations such as GDPR. It provides tools for data discovery, risk management, and data subject requests.

12. What is the purpose of the Microsoft Service Trust Portal?

A) To store large amounts of data

B) To develop software applications

C) To provide access to compliance resources and information

D) To manage network traffic

Correct Answer: C) To provide access to compliance resources and information.

Explanation: Microsoft Service Trust Portal provides access to compliance resources and information, including audit reports, compliance guides, and regulatory compliance information. It helps organizations understand and meet their compliance obligations.

13. What is the function of Microsoft Compliance Manager templates?

A) To increase data storage capacity

B) To manage network traffic

C) To develop software applications

D) To provide predefined assessments for specific regulations and standards

Correct Answer: D) To provide predefined assessments for specific regulations and standards.

Explanation: Microsoft Compliance Manager templates provide predefined assessments for specific regulations and standards, such as GDPR and ISO 27001. They help organizations evaluate their compliance posture and implement best practices to improve compliance.

14. What is the role of Microsoft Information Protection policies?

A) To store large amounts of data

B) To classify, label, and protect sensitive information based on its sensitivity

C) To develop software applications

D) To manage network traffic

Correct Answer: B) To classify, label, and protect sensitive information based on its sensitivity.

Explanation: Microsoft Information Protection policies help organizations classify, label, and protect sensitive information based on its sensitivity. They provide tools for applying protection policies, tracking data usage, and ensuring compliance with data protection regulations.

15. What is the purpose of Microsoft Communication Compliance?

      A) To store large amounts of data

      B) To monitor application performance

      C) To monitor and manage communications for compliance purposes

      D) To develop software applications

Correct Answer: C) To monitor and manage communications for compliance purposes.

Explanation: Microsoft Communication Compliance helps organizations monitor and manage communications for compliance purposes, ensuring that communications comply with regulatory requirements and internal policies. It provides tools for identifying and addressing compliance risks in communications.

16. What is the function of Microsoft Customer Lockbox?

      A) To increase data storage capacity

      B) To manage network traffic

      C) To provide customers with control over access to their data by Microsoft support engineers

      D) To develop software applications

Correct Answer: C) To provide customers with control over access to their data by Microsoft support engineers.

Explanation: Microsoft Customer Lockbox provides customers with control over access to their data by Microsoft support engineers, ensuring that customer data is accessed only with explicit approval. This helps maintain data privacy and compliance with data protection regulations.

17. What is the purpose of Microsoft Data Subject Requests (DSRs)?

A) To store large amounts of data
B) To help organizations respond to requests from individuals to access, correct, or delete their personal data
C) To develop software applications
D) To manage network traffic

Correct Answer: B) To help organizations respond to requests from individuals to access, correct, or delete their personal data.

Explanation: Microsoft Data Subject Requests (DSRs) help organizations respond to requests from individuals to access, correct, or delete their personal data, ensuring compliance with data protection regulations such as GDPR. They provide tools for managing and tracking DSRs.

18. What is the role of Microsoft Compliance Manager action items?

A) To provide specific tasks and recommendations for improving compliance posture
B) To manage network traffic
C) To increase data storage capacity
D) To develop software applications

Correct Answer: A) To provide specific tasks and recommendations for improving compliance posture.

Explanation: Microsoft Compliance Manager action items provide specific tasks and recommendations for improving an organization's compliance posture. They help organizations implement best practices and address compliance gaps identified in assessments.

19. What is the function of Microsoft Information Protection (MIP) sensitivity labels?

A) To store large amounts of data
B) To manage network traffic
C) To develop software applications
D) To classify and protect information based on its sensitivity

Correct Answer: D) To classify and protect information based on its sensitivity.

Explanation: Microsoft Information Protection (MIP) sensitivity labels help organizations classify and protect information based on its sensitivity. They provide tools for applying protection policies, tracking data usage, and ensuring compliance with data protection regulations.

20. What is the purpose of Microsoft Compliance Manager controls?

A) To provide specific security and compliance measures that organizations can implement
B) To develop software applications
C) To store large amounts of data
D) To manage network traffic

Correct Answer: A) To provide specific security and compliance measures that organizations can implement.

Explanation: Microsoft Compliance Manager controls provide specific security and compliance measures that organizations can implement to improve their compliance posture. They offer detailed guidance on how to implement and manage these controls effectively.

21. What is the role of Microsoft Compliance Manager assessments?

A) To increase data storage capacity
B) To manage network traffic
C) To evaluate an organization's compliance with specific regulations and standards
D) To develop software applications

Correct Answer: C) To evaluate an organization's compliance with specific regulations and standards.

Explanation: Microsoft Compliance Manager assessments evaluate an organization's compliance with specific regulations and standards, such as GDPR and ISO 27001. They provide a compliance score and actionable insights to help improve compliance and reduce risks.

22. What is the function of Microsoft Compliance Manager templates?

A) To provide predefined assessments for specific regulations and standards
B) To manage network traffic
C) To increase data storage capacity
D) To develop software applications

Correct Answer: A) To provide predefined assessments for specific regulations and standards.

Explanation: Microsoft Compliance Manager templates provide predefined assessments for specific regulations and standards, such as GDPR and ISO 27001. These templates help organizations evaluate their compliance posture and implement best practices to improve compliance.

23. What is the purpose of Microsoft Compliance Manager's compliance score?

A) To measure the effectiveness of security controls

B) To manage network traffic

C) To provide a quantifiable measure of an organization's compliance posture

D) To increase data storage capacity

Correct Answer: C) To provide a quantifiable measure of an organization's compliance posture.

Explanation: Microsoft Compliance Manager's compliance score provides a quantifiable measure of an organization's compliance posture by assessing its compliance with specific regulations and standards. This score helps organizations identify areas for improvement and track their progress over time.

24. What is Microsoft Data Classification?

A) A tool for encrypting data at rest

B) A method for developing software applications

C) A solution that helps identify and classify data based on its sensitivity

D) A service for managing network traffic

Correct Answer: C) A solution that helps identify and classify data based on its sensitivity.

Explanation: Microsoft Data Classification helps organizations identify and classify data based on its sensitivity. This classification enables organizations to apply appropriate protection policies and ensure compliance with data protection regulations.

25. What is the role of Microsoft Compliance Manager action items?

A) To provide specific tasks and recommendations for improving compliance posture

B) To manage network traffic

C) To increase data storage capacity

D) To develop software applications

Correct Answer: A) To provide specific tasks and recommendations for improving compliance posture.

Explanation: Microsoft Compliance Manager action items provide specific tasks and recommendations for improving an organization's compliance posture. These action items help organizations implement best practices and address compliance gaps identified in assessments.

Potential Interview Questions & Responses

1. What is the importance of multi-factor authentication (MFA)?

Multi-factor authentication (MFA) is crucial because it significantly enhances the security of user accounts by requiring multiple forms of verification before granting access. This added layer of security reduces the likelihood of unauthorized access, even if one authentication factor, such as a password, is compromised. For instance, an attacker would need to possess both the user's password and a second factor, such as a smartphone with an authentication app or a biometric signature, making it substantially harder to gain unauthorized entry. This practice is vital in protecting sensitive information and maintaining the integrity of organizational data.

2. Can you explain the concept of least privilege and its importance?

The principle of least privilege involves granting users the minimum level of access necessary to perform their job functions. This approach limits the potential damage from accidents, misuse, or malicious activities by restricting access to only those resources essential for a user's duties. For example, a marketing employee should not have access to financial systems or confidential data irrelevant to their role. By adhering to this principle, organizations can reduce the risk of internal threats and minimize the attack surface, thereby enhancing overall security posture.

3. How do you stay updated with the latest security threats and trends?

Staying updated with the latest security threats and trends requires a proactive approach, combining continuous learning and active community engagement. I regularly follow security news on reputable websites like Krebs on Security and Threatpost, which provide timely updates on emerging threats. Additionally, I participate in webinars and industry conferences such as DEFCON and Black Hat, which offer deep dives into current security challenges and innovations. Engaging with forums like the SANS Institute and Reddit's cybersecurity community also helps me stay connected with peers and industry experts, fostering a collaborative environment for knowledge sharing.

4. What steps would you take to respond to a security breach?

Responding to a security breach involves a systematic approach to minimize damage and restore normal operations. First, I would identify the breach using monitoring tools to determine the scope and impact. Next, I would contain the breach by isolating affected systems to prevent further damage. Once contained, I would eradicate the cause by removing any malicious software or unauthorized access. Following eradication, I would recover systems to normal operations, ensuring all data and services are restored securely. Finally, conducting a post-incident analysis is crucial to understand how the breach occurred and implement measures to prevent future incidents, including updating security policies and improving defense mechanisms.

5. What is the role of encryption in data security?

Encryption plays a fundamental role in data security by transforming readable data into an unreadable format using algorithms and encryption keys. This ensures that even if data is intercepted or accessed without authorization, it remains protected and unusable to unauthorized individuals. Encryption is critical for securing sensitive information such as financial transactions, personal data, and communications. For example, using SSL/TLS encryption for online transactions helps protect customer information from cybercriminals, maintaining confidentiality and integrity during data transmission.

6. Describe a time when you identified a security vulnerability and how you addressed it.

During my previous role as an intern, I identified a security vulnerability in our web application related to SQL injection attacks. After thorough analysis, I documented the findings and proposed implementing prepared statements and parameterized queries to mitigate the risk. Collaborating closely with the development team, we implemented these changes and conducted extensive follow-up testing to ensure the vulnerability was resolved. This proactive approach not only secured our application but also demonstrated the importance of continuous monitoring and timely intervention in maintaining robust security.

7. What is a security policy, and why is it important?

A security policy is a formal document that outlines how an organization will protect its information technology assets and data. It includes guidelines on access control, data protection, incident response, and employee responsibilities. Security policies are crucial as they provide a structured framework for consistent and effective security practices, helping organizations meet regulatory requirements and mitigate risks. For instance, a comprehensive security policy can define how employees should handle sensitive data, ensuring adherence to best practices and compliance with legal standards.

8. How do you manage access control in a networked environment?

Managing access control in a networked environment involves implementing multiple methods to ensure that only authorized users can access specific resources. This includes employing role-based access control (RBAC) to assign permissions based on user roles, using access control lists (ACLs) to define which users or systems can access specific resources, and leveraging identity and access management (IAM) solutions like Microsoft Entra ID to manage identities and enforce access policies. Regular audits are also essential to review access permissions and ensure they remain appropriate and secure, adapting to changes in roles and responsibilities within the organization.

9. What is the significance of compliance in cybersecurity?

Compliance in cybersecurity ensures that an organization adheres to laws, regulations, and standards designed to protect data privacy and security. This is significant because non-compliance can lead to severe consequences, including legal penalties, financial losses, and reputational damage. Compliance frameworks such as GDPR, HIPAA, and ISO/IEC 27001 provide guidelines for implementing robust security measures and maintaining accountability. Adhering to these standards not only protects the organization but also builds trust with customers and stakeholders by demonstrating a commitment to data protection and ethical practices.

10. Can you explain the concept of a Security Operations Center (SOC)?

A Security Operations Center (SOC) is a centralized unit that handles security issues at an organizational level. The SOC team is responsible for monitoring, detecting, analyzing, and responding to security incidents using a combination of technology solutions and human expertise. The primary goal of a SOC is to identify and mitigate threats in real-time, ensuring the organization's IT infrastructure remains secure. By providing continuous monitoring and a coordinated response to incidents, a SOC helps protect sensitive data, prevent breaches, and maintain the overall security posture of the organization.

11. What tools and technologies are you familiar with for identity management?

I am familiar with several tools and technologies for identity management, including Microsoft Entra ID, Okta,

Azure Active Directory (Azure AD), and Ping Identity. Microsoft Entra ID is particularly effective for managing identities and access in cloud environments, providing robust authentication and authorization capabilities. Okta is a cloud-based IAM solution known for its ease of integration and comprehensive access management features. Azure AD is essential for identity management within Microsoft Azure, offering seamless integration with other Microsoft services. Ping Identity provides enterprise-grade identity management and single sign-on (SSO) solutions, ensuring secure and efficient access across multiple applications.

12. What are the key components of a disaster recovery plan?

A disaster recovery plan (DRP) includes several key components to ensure business continuity in the event of a disruption. First, a risk assessment identifies potential threats and their impact on operations. This is followed by a business impact analysis (BIA) to determine critical business functions and the resources required to support them. Recovery strategies are then developed to outline procedures for restoring systems and data. Clearly defined roles and responsibilities are assigned to ensure effective execution of the plan. Regular testing and maintenance are crucial to validate the plan's effectiveness and update it as needed, ensuring preparedness for various disaster scenarios.

13. How would you handle a situation where an employee is found to be violating security policies?

Handling a situation where an employee violates security policies involves several steps to address the issue and prevent recurrence. Initially, it is important to respond promptly by investigating the extent of the violation and mitigating any immediate risks. Documentation of the incident is crucial for review and future reference. Educating the employee about the importance of security policies and providing additional training can help prevent similar incidents. If necessary, disciplinary measures should be applied according to the organization's policies. This approach not only addresses the current issue but also reinforces the significance of adhering to security policies.

14. What are some common indicators of a phishing attack?

Common indicators of a phishing attack include emails from suspicious or unknown senders, urgent language that creates a sense of fear or urgency, and unexpected attachments that could contain malware. Phishing emails often contain links to fake websites designed to steal sensitive information, with URLs that do not match the legitimate site or contain misspellings. Requests for personal or financial information are also common in phishing attempts. Recognizing these signs is crucial in preventing phishing attacks and protecting sensitive data from being compromised.

15. Can you explain the difference between vulnerability assessment and penetration testing?

Vulnerability assessment and penetration testing are both critical components of a comprehensive security strategy, but they serve different purposes. A vulnerability assessment is a process that identifies and classifies security vulnerabilities in a system using automated tools to scan for known weaknesses. It provides a report on potential issues that need to be addressed. Penetration testing, on the other hand, involves a simulated cyber attack to exploit vulnerabilities actively. It goes beyond identification by testing the effectiveness of security controls and providing insights into how an attacker could gain unauthorized access. Together, these methods help ensure robust security by identifying and mitigating potential risks.

16. What is role-based access control (RBAC) and its benefits?

Role-based access control (RBAC) is a method of managing access to resources based on user roles within an organization. Each role is assigned specific permissions that align with job responsibilities, ensuring that users only have access to the resources necessary for their duties. RBAC simplifies administration by making it easier to manage access by roles rather than individual users. It improves security by reducing the risk of unauthorized access and enhances compliance by providing clear access control policies. For example, an HR manager would have access to employee records, while an IT administrator would have access to system configurations.

17. How would you ensure the security of a cloud environment?

Ensuring the security of a cloud environment involves a multi-faceted approach. Firstly, implementing robust identity and access management (IAM) practices is crucial, such as using multi-factor authentication (MFA) and role-based access control (RBAC) to restrict access to resources. Secondly, encryption must be employed both for data at rest and in transit to protect sensitive information. Regularly updating and patching systems to mitigate vulnerabilities is essential. Additionally, using security tools like cloud security posture management (CSPM) solutions can continuously monitor and manage the cloud security posture. Finally, conducting regular security audits and penetration testing helps identify and address potential weaknesses.

18. What is a data breach, and what steps should be taken following one?

A data breach is an incident where sensitive, protected, or confidential data is accessed, disclosed, or stolen by an unauthorized individual. Following a data breach, the first step is to identify and contain the breach to prevent further data loss. This is followed by eradicating the root cause, such as removing malware or closing exploited vulnerabilities. After containment and eradication, recovering any compromised systems and data is crucial. Communication is vital, so informing stakeholders, regulatory bodies, and affected individuals promptly is necessary. Finally, conducting a post-incident analysis helps to understand how the breach occurred and to implement measures to prevent future breaches.

19. Can you explain the concept of zero trust security?

Zero trust security is a security model based on the principle of "never trust, always verify." Unlike traditional security models that rely on perimeter defenses, zero trust assumes that threats can come from inside and outside the network. Therefore, it requires continuous verification of every request for access to resources, regardless of its origin. This involves strict identity verification, device security checks, and least privilege access controls. By minimizing trust and continuously validating all interactions, zero trust helps protect against modern cyber threats and minimizes the risk of unauthorized access.

20. How do you conduct a security risk assessment?

Conducting a security risk assessment involves several steps. Firstly, identifying the assets that need protection, such as data, systems, and networks, is essential. Next, identifying potential threats and vulnerabilities that could impact these assets is crucial. Assessing the likelihood and impact of each identified threat helps prioritize risks. Following this, implementing appropriate security controls to mitigate identified risks is necessary. Finally, continuously monitoring and reviewing the security posture to adapt to new threats and changes in the environment is essential. Documentation and regular updates to the risk assessment ensure it remains relevant and effective.

21. What is the role of security awareness training in an organization?

Security awareness training is vital for educating employees about cybersecurity threats and best practices to mitigate them. It helps create a security-conscious culture where employees are vigilant and proactive in identifying and responding to potential threats. Training covers topics such as recognizing phishing attempts, using strong passwords, securing personal devices, and understanding data protection policies. By empowering employees with knowledge and skills, security awareness training reduces the risk of human error, enhances overall security posture, and ensures compliance with regulatory requirements.

22. How do you handle sensitive data to ensure it is protected?

Handling sensitive data involves implementing several security measures to ensure its protection. Encrypting data both at rest and in transit is fundamental to protect it from unauthorized access. Access to sensitive data should be restricted using role-based access control (RBAC), ensuring only authorized personnel have access. Regularly updating and patching systems and applications helps mitigate vulnerabilities. Additionally, implementing data loss prevention (DLP) tools can monitor and control data transfers to prevent unauthorized sharing or leakage. Finally, conducting regular audits and security assessments ensures that data protection measures are effective and up-to-date.

23. What is the importance of incident response planning?

Incident response planning is crucial for effectively managing and mitigating the impact of security incidents. It provides a structured approach for identifying, responding to, and recovering from incidents. An incident response plan (IRP) helps ensure that incidents are handled promptly and efficiently, minimizing damage and restoring normal operations quickly. Key components of an IRP include defining roles and responsibilities, establishing communication protocols, and outlining specific procedures for different types of incidents. Regular testing and updating of the plan ensure its effectiveness and preparedness for real-world scenarios.

24. How do you approach securing mobile devices in an enterprise environment?

Securing mobile devices in an enterprise environment involves implementing several strategies. Firstly, using mobile device management (MDM) solutions helps enforce security policies, such as requiring device encryption and enabling remote wipe capabilities. Implementing strong authentication methods, such as MFA, ensures that only authorized users can access corporate resources. Regularly updating and patching mobile operating systems and applications is crucial to mitigate vulnerabilities. Educating employees about the risks associated with mobile devices and best practices for secure usage is also essential. Additionally, monitoring and managing mobile device activity helps detect and respond to potential security threats.

25. Can you explain the concept of a security perimeter and its relevance today?

The concept of a security perimeter refers to the traditional approach of securing an organization's network by establishing a boundary between the internal network and external threats. This typically involves using firewalls, intrusion detection systems (IDS), and other perimeter defenses to protect against external attacks. However, with the rise of cloud computing, mobile devices, and remote work, the traditional security perimeter has become less relevant. Today's security strategies focus more on protecting data and resources wherever they are located, using concepts like zero trust and identity-centric security to ensure robust protection in a perimeter-less environment.

26. What measures can be taken to protect against insider threats?

Protecting against insider threats involves implementing several measures. Firstly, enforcing strict access controls and using the principle of least privilege ensures that employees only have access to the resources necessary for their roles. Monitoring and auditing user activity helps detect unusual behavior that may indicate insider threats. Implementing data loss prevention (DLP) tools can prevent unauthorized data transfers. Conducting regular security awareness training educates employees about the risks and signs of insider threats. Additionally, having a robust incident response plan in place ensures that any suspected insider threats are addressed promptly and effectively.

Summary of the Book and Exam Preparation

This comprehensive guide provides a detailed roadmap to mastering the Microsoft SC-900 exam, which certifies foundational knowledge in Security, Compliance, and Identity within Microsoft's ecosystem. The book is meticulously structured to cover the key areas of the exam, ensuring a thorough understanding of each domain.

1. Describe the Concepts of Security, Compliance, and Identity (10-15%):

This section introduces the fundamental principles of security, compliance, and identity management. It explains the importance of protecting data and systems, adhering to regulatory requirements, and managing user identities. Practical examples include implementing firewalls, encryption, and access controls.

2. Describe the Capabilities of Microsoft Entra (25-30%):

Focusing on Microsoft Entra, this section delves into its identity and access management capabilities. You'll learn about authentication methods (passwords, biometrics, MFA), access management (Conditional Access, RBAC), and identity protection features (Privileged Identity Management, Entra ID Governance).

3. Describe the Capabilities of Microsoft Security Solutions (35-40%):

This extensive section covers Microsoft's security solutions. It explores core infrastructure security services like Azure DDoS Protection, Azure Firewall, and Web Application Firewall (WAF). Additionally, it discusses security management capabilities through Microsoft Defender for Cloud, Cloud Security Posture Management (CSPM), and threat detection and response with Microsoft Sentinel and Defender XDR.

4. Describe the Capabilities of Microsoft Compliance Solutions (20-25%):

Here, you'll understand the tools and resources Microsoft provides to ensure compliance. The section covers the Microsoft Service Trust Portal, Microsoft Purview Compliance Manager, data governance solutions, data classification, sensitivity labels, and data loss prevention (DLP).

Exam Preparation Tips:

Days Leading Up to the Exam:

1. Review Key Concepts: Go over each section covered in this book. Focus on understanding the principles rather than rote memorization.

2. Practice with Sample Questions: Engage with practice exams and scenario-based questions to familiarize yourself with the exam format and question types.

3. Join Study Groups: Collaborate with peers who are also preparing for the SC-900 exam. Study groups can provide support, additional insights, and motivation.

4. Use Microsoft Learn Resources: Take advantage of free resources and training modules available on Microsoft Learn. These are specifically designed to help you prepare for Microsoft certifications.

On the Exam Day:

1. Stay Calm and Confident: Trust in the preparation you've done. Stay positive and confident in your knowledge and abilities.

2. Read Questions Carefully: Take your time to read each question thoroughly before answering. Pay attention to details in scenario-based questions.

3. Manage Your Time: Keep an eye on the clock to ensure you have ample time to complete all questions. Don't spend too much time on any one question.

4. Review Your Answers: If time permits, review your answers to ensure you haven't missed any details or made any mistakes.

Final Encouragement:

You have put in the hard work and dedication to prepare for the Microsoft SC-900 exam. This book has equipped you with the knowledge and tools needed to succeed. Approach the exam with confidence, knowing that you have a solid understanding of the core concepts and practical applications.

Remember, passing the SC-900 exam is a significant step forward in your career in security, compliance, and identity management. It validates your skills and knowledge, opening doors to new opportunities and advancements.

I wish you the best of luck on your exam day. Keep striving for excellence and continue to acquire more knowledge to add value to your career. Your commitment to learning and professional growth will undoubtedly lead to success.

www.ingramcontent.com/pod-product-compliance
Lightning Source LLC
Chambersburg PA
CBHW060151060326
40690CB00018B/4064